M000120441

# Fermented Foods

# Fermented Foods

*The History and Science
of a Microbiological Wonder*

CHRISTINE BAUMGARTHUBER

REAKTION BOOKS

*For E.B.M. and H.P.L.*

Published by
REAKTION BOOKS LTD
Unit 32, Waterside
44–48 Wharf Road
London N1 7UX, UK
www.reaktionbooks.co.uk

First published 2021
Copyright © Christine Baumgarthuber 2021

Printed and bound in Great Britain
by TJ Books Ltd, Padstow, Cornwall

A catalogue record for this book is available from
the British Library

ISBN 978 1 78914 375 1

# Contents

# Introduction
# Faithful Friends and
# Implacable Foes:
# *The Nature and History of*
# *Our Relationship to Microbes*

The versatile character of the microbe is strikingly revealed
in the contemplation of the kaleidoscopic mosaic of life.
– Arthur Isaac Kendall, *Civilization and the Microbe* (1923)[1]

IN THE SPRING OF 2007, I received a small envelope containing
a sourdough starter born on the Oregon Trail, a survival of
American pioneers' push westward. The starter could not have been
more unprepossessing. It looked like dust and left me wondering
whether I had erred in ordering it. I nevertheless mixed it with
flour and spring water in a Mason jar and went to bed, only to wake
to a bubbling goo that covered the countertop. As I cleaned up the
mess it came home to me how much livelier than store-bought
dried yeast this heirloom starter was.

The starter had a personality, and a finicky one at that. It sulked
when I left it unused in the refrigerator too long. And it sulked
even more when I forced on it rice flour and tapioca during a
gluten-free diet lark I went on for a few months. Really, even
keeping the thermostat too low in winter put it out of temper. Its
spirits would rise with the arrival of spring. The warmer days set
it enthusiastically digesting the organic rye flour I fed it, and it

would reward my care with perfect loaves of crispy French bread, airy ciabatta and dense rounds of sour rye.

My success with it inspired me to attempt other ferments. For guidance I turned to Sandor Ellix Katz's seminal *Wild Fermentation* and my family of ferments came to include, at various times, kefir, kombucha, lactic-acid-fermented cucumbers, beetroot and peppers, as well as *tibicos* (a fermented drink popular in Mexico), cider and even red wine.

Each evening I tended my ferments, the ritual anchoring me in what I saw as an increasingly tumultuous world. Financial markets might have been crashing along with my prospects of a steady job, but I could care for my ferments, each one a world in itself, and I would be rewarded with health and a hobby. George Orwell thought taking tea to be a mainstay of civilization. For me it was brewing tea for another batch of kombucha.

I suspect my motivation for taking up fermenting differed little from urges felt by others who take up keeping chickens, putting up preserves and similar 'urban homesteading' pursuits. I sought connection to a sweep of time vaster than my own moment. For ages ordinary people have brewed beer, ripened cheese, baked bread and cured meats in times of war and of peace, of plenty and of want. Only quite recently in history has the art come to be seen as arcane, even dicey.

I have been told home fermenting is a waste of time. I have also been told that I will probably poison myself. These dismissive if not distrustful remarks led me to ask why it is that do-it-yourself fermenting no longer seems to enjoy the same aura of cosy self-sufficiency as, say, baking pies from scratch. The answer, I was to discover, is an important part of this history of fermented foods. As it turns out, suspicion of fermented foods owes to a peculiar blend of scientific and market forces so influential as to sway consumer preference in the direction of bland, unappetizing mass-produced substitutes for the zestier originals we can – and did – make ourselves. Fermented foods reflect humanity's relationship to a second domain of life both invisible and ubiquitous. Their history is a history of how we came to learn that bacteria and fungi are our friends and foes, variously. The danger we imagine homemade sauerkraut or sausage to pose, then, rests on our awareness of how fell an unseen enemy can be – and did indeed prove to be one fateful Scottish summer nearly a century ago.

\* \* \*

August 1922 saw the death of eight visitors to a hotel in the remote western Scottish Highlands known for its romantic scenery and excellent management. None of the eight appeared frail or unwell. On 14 August they had gone on an excursion planned for them by the hotel staff. That morning each went his own way – some to fish, others to mountaineer – before convening on the shore of nearby Loch Maree for a lunch of sandwiches of pâtés of wild duck, ham and beef tongue, along with jam, butter, hard-boiled eggs, scones and cake. Everyone in the party returned to the hotel in time for dinner.

The next morning a guest who went on the excursion, one 'Mr S.', began vomiting. By the evening of that day he had died.

Another guest, one 'Mr W.', fared little better. Dizzy when he woke, he staggered when he tried to walk and complained of double vision. He summoned a doctor, to whom he apologized for having put him to any trouble. Then, feeling somewhat better, he went to breakfast. The next morning found him paralysed, and by the evening of that same day he, too, had died.

Also suffering from double vision was 'Mr T.', at 22 years old the youngest victim. Though his symptoms were mild early on, by the morning of 16 August he could no longer speak and was dead by the afternoon.

'Mr D.' likewise woke to dizziness and double vision on the morning of 15 August. Rather than take to bed, however, he boarded his boat. He rowed four miles, remarking to his boatman at one point that he would see two fish for every one that would appear. The following day saw him neither better nor worse, save that his double vision had gone. The next day it was back, and his speech was slurred as well. Things continued this way for two more days. On Sunday 20 August, paralysis gripped him. Death claimed him by noon of the following day.

The four other guests similarly died following bouts of dizziness, double vision and finally paralysis. Physicians present suspected food poisoning. But of what kind? Because the toxin claimed two boatmen, they must have dined at some point with the remaining victims, all hotel guests. While they could still manage, several victims had mentioned the excursion and its al fresco luncheon. Suspicion fell on the duck pâté.

Official inquiries began. Foodstuffs from the hotel were sent away for bacteriological examination. The cook was interviewed. On 30 June, six weeks before the tragedy, there had arrived at the hotel two dozen containers of potted meat from one of the finest manufacturers in the county. Indeed, the manufacturer had observed every precaution at each stage of the meat's preparation. Workers cooked the meat in bulk, canned it, put the open cans in retorts for sterilizing and then in small glass containers for a second boiling. A million jars had been made according to this process and not a single incident of poisoning had been reported prior to the event at the Loch Maree hotel. The cook attested that the jars had arrived in pristine condition, and when opened their contents neither looked nor smelled spoilt.

Too little pâté remained in the jars to allow for thorough analysis. Yet as luck would have it investigators unearthed (quite literally) another source: a sandwich in a garden bed, buried there by a boatman who had saved it from the earlier excursion picnic to have for supper only to be sickened by it. Word had got to him that possibly tainted duck pâté was to blame for the recent rash of illness. Thus the burial was to protect his hens, which he thought might die had he simply thrown away the sandwich and they discovered it. The sandwich was duly dug up, sent for analysis and revealed to be tainted – indeed, thoroughly so.

The terrible toxin, which could survive multiple bouts of sterilization and boiling, not to mention burial and exhumation, baffled authorities. A press release issued on 25 August by the Scottish Board of Health acknowledged the mystery surrounding the poisonings but urged the public to remain calm.[2] Investigators had managed to isolate an organism from the duck pâté. They injected a broth culture of it into two mice. Both died, as did a rabbit they had also injected. A bacteriologist noted that rabbit and mice alike developed symptoms characteristic of botulism.[3]

\* \* \*

An anaerobic, rod-shaped, spore-releasing bacterium that thrives where no other bacteria may, *Clostridium botulinum* secretes a powerful biological toxin that targets the peripheral nervous system. This toxin is present only when the bacteria release their spores. These spores are amazingly hardy, however, living in everything from garden soil to the gills of salmon and through everything from extreme cold, heat and radiation to vast stretches of time.[4] The first individual to identify the tough *C. botulinum* microbe was Belgian bacteriologist Émile van Ermengem. In 1895, during his search for a cause for a rash of sausage- and cured meat-related poisonings, he isolated a microorganism not easily eradicated – one that would endure as a killer foodborne disease to the present day.[5]

A judicial inquiry ruled *C. botulinum* the lone culprit in the Loch Maree poisonings, which happened to occur at a time when blame fell on microorganisms for nearly every illness. Microorganisms and their workings, helpful and harmful, had entered the awareness of ordinary men and women by way of the hygienic movement, whose 'golden era' ran from the late nineteenth century

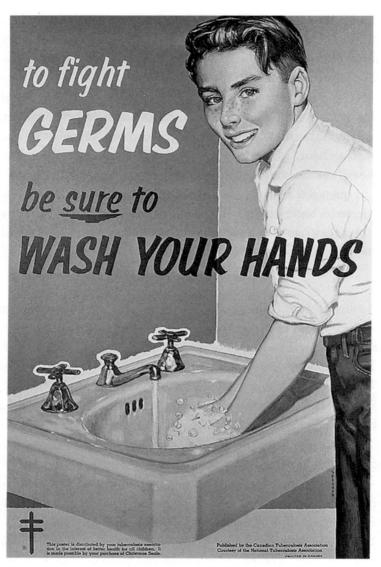

to fight GERMS be <u>sure</u> to WASH YOUR HANDS

This poster is distributed by your tuberculosis association in the interest of better health for all children. It is made possible by your purchase of Christmas Seals.

Published by the Canadian Tuberculosis Association
Courtesy of the National Tuberculosis Association
PRINTED IN CANADA

Print advertisement issued by the Canadian Tuberculosis Association for the promotion of proper personal cleanliness, 1959. Advances in the 19th and 20th centuries led to a better understanding of the role played by microorganisms in human illness. Unfortunately, the period also saw trust in traditional fermentation practices falter.

to 1930 or so. Characterized by a concern with the spread of tuberculosis, typhoid and other so-called diseases of filth, the movement grew alongside better understanding of the agents of such disease. It waged public health campaigns dedicated to increasing awareness of the relationship between microbes and disease. Prior to this development, such awareness remained confined to laboratories and factories; ordinary people knew little of the biological processes behind the beer they drank, the cheese they ate or the misery they suffered from a dodgy pâté. They likely did have inklings, borne of observation and conventional wisdom, as to why foods handled one way might bring sensual pleasure and health, and foods handled another way, illness and death. Yet the methods were so deeply woven in the folkways of their community as to defy explanation.

The public health campaigns would spring knowledge of microorganisms and their effects from various regional idioms and deposit it in a form accessible to almost everyone.[6] From presses issued home-economics books and pamphlets bringing word of 'germ theory', as the new science became known, to kitchens of every class and urging more hygienic ways of cooking on housewives.[7] All good practices, to be sure. Yet the campaigns also epitomized the tyranny of good intentions, as common domestic activities came to acquire an aura of unseen danger. 'No viper so little, but hath its venom' – the adage was never so fitting.

Never mind that for centuries home-made pickles, wines and buttermilks had been made without incident. Now people knew that microbes had lurked everywhere all the while, invisibly awaiting the merest lapse in cleanliness. At once imperceptible and ever present, the risk of microbial contamination stoked unease enough among housewives to drive them into the waiting arms of food industrialists and their retail auxiliaries, store proprietors: the first making and the second stocking factory-made, hygienically packed versions of foods formerly prepared at home.

For a time the old ways of fermenting food coexisted with the new. Beer bottled in modern state-of-the-art breweries and cheese made in factories shared shelves with cucumbers pickled and bread baked at home. But as the nineteenth century rolled into the twentieth, the railways brought new foodstuffs to market and radio brought them to people's attention. They, and only they, were reliably clean and healthy – or so the large companies that made them sought to convince the public. The persuasive campaign was helped by passage of the United States Congress's Pure Food and Drug Act of 1906, which was patterned after the British Parliament's Sale of Foods and Drugs Act of 1875 and Margarine Act of 1887. Only well-capitalized enterprises could invest in the equipment necessary for meeting the new standards and win the governmental seal of approval to which consumers came to look for assurance. The seal became prohibitively expensive to win; smaller manufacturers saw their customer base shrink and were soon bankrupted.

Their success having bred in them a desire for more, corporations doubled down on their claim that they alone supplied healthy food. Domino Sugar made the case that food produced by mechanical processes was cleaner and therefore safer than food made by human hands. Gold Medal Flour touted their product as untouched by any miller, and Kellogg's promoted their 'Waxtite' cereal box packaging as contamination-proof. Heinz invited the public into select areas of its factories to gawk at the virginal women dressed in white who packed the company's pickles.[8]

Large companies' advertising efforts consisted of such stunts, which often pushed past sensationalism into shamelessness. Eager for an edge in a national market, the American Sugar Refining Company ran adverts that featured enlarged images of harmless yet frightening-looking brown sugar microbes as evidence of the dangers of eating unrefined sugar. The campaign succeeded so thoroughly that even the best-selling *Boston Cooking-school Cook*

An early 20th-century print advertisement for Kellogg's Corn Flakes breakfast cereal. The added packaging feature of a 'Waxtite' wrapper was inspired by advances in microbiology of the time. There came to prevail the notion that food safety and purity depended on food's isolation from any possible contaminants. Yet, like so many other things in industrial capitalism, such safety and purity remained less a matter of fact than perception, which industrial food manufacturers assiduously cultivated in consumers.

*Book* warned readers off brown sugar for reason of 'a minute insect' that lurked within it.[9]

The breakfast cereal and biscuit industries soon followed suit. Companies claimed that only packaged cereals were guaranteed to be free of germs. A meat-and-egg breakfast teemed with possible ill health, as did yeast-risen bread. Safer and more wholesome by far were 'Toasted Corn Flakes' manufactured according to the highest standards of hygiene. For biscuit manufacturers the enemy was that fixture of country stores, the cracker barrel. These were likewise cesspools of germs, their contents bought in wholesale and dumped into barrels of dubious cleanliness only to be grubbed out again by equally dubious hands. Nabisco offered instead individually wrapped, sanitary packages of crackers that appeared to have been touched by no one.[10]

The appearance of purity was about the only thing going for these mass-produced edibles. (Many of the large food factories would stage simulacra of ideal production conditions for curious visitors, as the far less tidy real production went on elsewhere.) They were otherwise boringly bland and uniform, lacking the terroir of traditional foods. 'I have heard the American kitchen is miserable,' said Czar Nicholas of Russia to one of his subjects, an opera singer who had recently visited the United States. 'All the foods are prepared on a big scale and they have no individual taste or flavour.'[11]

This judgement held true for mass-produced food in Europe and Britain as well. The time-pressed working classes of industrial cities such as Manchester and Aberdeen forsook watercress, fish and other traditional foods for tinned beef and Bird's custard from a mix, for processed foods were easier to eat in the few free hours they had.[12] As it turned out, what time labourers saved they later lost: their life expectancy decreased and they fell victim in greater numbers to scurvy, tooth decay and other degenerative diseases.

In Switzerland, industrial food pioneer Julius Maggi convinced housewives to adopt the dried bouillon cubes he had perfected.

Though they lacked the savour and nutrition of home-made stock, they appealed to modern women, many of whom had jobs outside the home. They were such a success that in 1897 Maggi founded his eponymous company in Germany. Convenience had evidently trumped taste, the relentless, inflexible rhythm of the factory having reshaped domestic priorities. Time spent on cooking was time not spent in working for pay. Also, industrialization had made food cheaper and this gave reason for optimism. 'Daily, the great factories will deliver tasty, freshly prepared and cooked food at

An early 20th-century Dutch print advertisement for Maggi's bouillon cubes. (The tagline reads, '. . . the real brand!') As with any industrial food, Maggi's bouillon saved harried homemakers time in meal preparation, but such convenience came at the expense of nutrition and savour.

very low prices,' proclaimed Auguste Corthay, industrialist and erstwhile chef to Umberto 1 of Italy, sometime in the 1890s. 'It will be the start of a new century!'[13]

The start of a new century it was. The hygiene movement marked a watershed in food production and preservation – for better and for worse. It taught ordinary people simple ways of preventing horrific diseases. And though they became healthier and less prone to illness, they also surrendered to government and big business considerable autonomy in domestic and culinary affairs. Absolute and monolithic in its prescriptions and predictions, the hygiene movement's discourse left little room for idiosyncrasy or traditional wisdom in terms of humankind's relationship to microorganisms.

\* \* \*

Traditional wisdom, whose rough, culturally specific recommendations summoned forth in those who followed it a kind of inventiveness in making do, had been supplanted by a rigid set of rules predicated on fear. (This is why today knowledge of how to avoid colds is more common than knowledge of how to bake sourdough bread or pickle carrots.) This fear, as incidents such as that at Loch Maree showed, was not unfounded. Whether bacteria, yeast or mould, these tiny Janus-faced creatures could bring illness or health. 'Society is not made up just of men, for everywhere microbes intervene and act,' wrote the contemporary French sociologist Bruno Latour in his *Pasteurization of France*.[14] Who could discern the aims of these shadowy agents?

Before the modern era, no one could. For understanding the dual character of microorganisms requires knowing something about their biology. A microorganism is simply any organism too small to be seen with the naked eye. Indeed, a million (or more!) may fit on the head of a pin.[15] How they came to be is a tale as old as time. Microorganisms spent aeons awaiting their human foils,

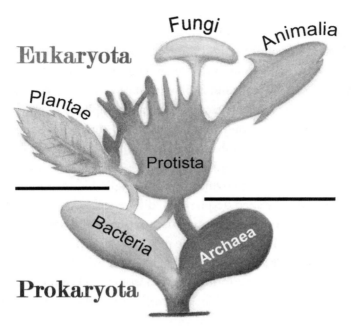

A schematic illustration depicting the evolution of life from lower to higher forms. The kingdoms of living things today owe their existence to a primordial symbiogenesis between bacteria and archaea in the remote past. The event not only made higher forms of life possible, but helped to make the planet hospitable to many of them.

and they will likely endure for aeons more once humans disappear. They arose some 4 billion years ago. Not at all the hospitable, largely temperate world we call home, Earth then was a planet buffeted by comets, meteors and solar radiation. Added to these assaults were violent tidal surges caused by the gravitational pull of a moon that orbited fifteen times nearer than it does today. Beneath the roiling seas hydrothermal vents released immense heat generated by the Earth's core. Surrounding these vents were accumulations of mud rich in matter essential for life, which, as the pioneering British science-fiction writer H. G. Wells wrote, was but 'a little glow, scarcely kindled yet, in these void immensities'.[16]

Scarcely kindled yet extant nonetheless, life in the form of primitive cells took hold, multiplying and diversifying even as earth went from hot to frigid some 2 billion years ago. They would evolve into two distinct unicellular types, bacteria and archaea. Bacteria have cell walls but lack organelles and an organized nucleus. Archaea are like bacteria in size and simplicity of structure, but, unlike bacteria, they possess genes and metabolic pathways that more closely resemble life forms of far greater complexity. And though bacteria and archaea alike draw on the sun's energy, the latter prefer environments inhospitable to the former. Some affinity obtained despite such differences; according to the prevailing theory of symbiogenesis, archaea assimilated bacteria without destroying them at some point, the two merging to form eukaryotes – cells and organisms that have a clearly defined nucleus containing DNA in the form of chromosomes.[17] (We humans are eukaryotes.) This new symbiotic form, by virtue of the extra energy provided by the bacteria, could grow larger, accumulate more genes and become more complex.[18] There evolved strains whose waste product, oxygen, would establish conditions in which life could begin to diversify on a grand scale.

Microorganisms now live everywhere and play a role in every biological process. They maintain the world's ecosystems and contribute to the health of the organisms that live within those systems.[19] They decompose dead things and succour living. And when it suits them, they bring disease, famine and death.

And in that remote past some 2 billion years ago was set the stage for humankind's eventual engagement with these early life forms. Some 39 trillion microbes live within us. We understand the roles and responsibilities of only a fraction.[20] Still, we know that many of them enhance our immune system, balance our blood sugar, improve digestion and make other helpful contributions to our health and well-being. On our part, we have manipulated microorganisms to increase our food supply and make it more

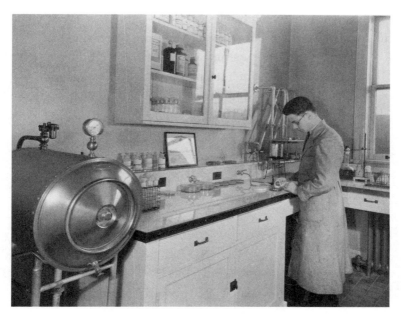

Dearborn Chemical Company's bacteriological analysis laboratory in Chicago, Illinois, c. 1930. Science of the early and mid-20th century took a rather alarmist view of microorganisms, much to the detriment of age-old fermentation methods. Yet recent decades have seen renewed interest in the roles microorganisms play in our health, longevity and well-being.

nutritious and palatable, domesticating them as we domesticated cattle and sheep to feed our workers, soldiers and idle rich alike.

What purpose, however, do we serve for them? This unsettling question remains unanswered, for the motives of these invisible life forms remain obscure. They 'infest all our surroundings and have such an extraordinary potentiality for good or evil', observed Professor Percy F. Frankland in 1891, 'appearing sometimes as our friends and faithful servants doing the work which they are bidden without a murmur, whilst at other times they oppose us as implacable foes and defy our power and ingenuity'.[21] We have spent just as much energy fighting those microbes that cause disease and death and which spoil the fruits of our labour as we have in cultivating those which bring health and happiness. We struggle to domesticate microbes to keep them from colonizing us.

Happily, this ceaseless struggle has made, as the British novelist Thomas Hardy wrote, for 'rattling good history' – and not a few tasty morsels besides.[22] But before we tuck into these morsels, we should think about drinks. After all, some of the earliest ferments, perhaps unsurprisingly, came in the form of heady brews.

# 1 Laughter and Wild Play: *The Birth and Evolution of Fermented Drink*

A Book of Verses underneath the Bough,
A Jug of Wine, a Loaf of Bread – and Thou
Beside me singing in the Wilderness –
Oh, Wilderness were Paradise enow!
– *Rubáiyát of Omar Khayyám*[1]

THOUGH IT REMAINS UNKNOWN how humankind discovered alcoholic beverages, it was almost certainly by accident.

The first were fruit ferments, naturally; they needed no coaxing. Every wasp buzzing in an orchard or around a puddle of spilled soft drink carries in it countless yeast cells. Whenever it eats or defecates, it introduces these cells to the sugary substance. Before long their enzymes turn the sugars into ethyl alcohol.

Turning sugars into alcohol is an ability yeast developed some 100 million years ago. The prevailing theory holds that yeast cells suspended in tree sap began to mate. Their commingling set off a genetic eruption known as 'whole genome duplication'. When it was complete it enabled yeast to turn glucose into alcohol.[2] (This process of gene duplication is important for evolution because it allows the replicas of genes to take on new functions.[3]) In one of those happy accidents that sometimes occur in nature, the same genome duplication happened to the Cretaceous ancestors of flowering plants that evolved to produce fleshy, sweet fruit preferred by yeast. Some 63 million years later, humans would find a source of solace and inspiration in the product of this meeting of food and feeder – alcohol – when a daring soul likely sampled some fermented fruit pulp and found the effect it wrought quite pleasant.

Others later observed that milk and water mixed with honey also fermented into intoxicating beverages. Through trial and error a process was developed over time whereby such beverages could be created more or less reliably. Grapes proved an especially suitable fermentable source, and thus wine was born. Development of beer, a more difficult beverage to make, would take longer; unlike fruit, milk or honey-infused water, cereal grains come wrapped in a tough husk and contain starches and sugars that yeast cannot access.

In time, human ingenuity prevailed. The key lay in converting grains' starches and sugars from insoluble to soluble, which required the presence of an enzyme. Ptyalin, a starch-converting amylase, occurs in saliva, and the act of chewing serves as the means of introducing it to grain. To this day makers of South American chicha chew corn to ferment this beloved traditional beer. A second class of enzyme suited to the task, diastase, results from sprouting, or 'malting', grain. Heated in water in a process called mashing, the malted grain produces a sugar- and enzyme-rich liquid that readily ferments into alcohol.

Mashing remains alive and well among the peoples of Africa. The variety of beers brewed by them range from fizzy liquid to a runny gruel. Yet despite differences in consistency they all contain a mixture of acids and alcohols, by-products of the yeasts and lactic acid bacteria present during the process. The *pito* of the Nigerian Bini people, for example, derives from malted maize and sorghum, which are sprouted in baskets lined with banana leaves. The sprouted grain is ground, boiled, cooled, strained and left

A bowl of chicha prepared for celebration of the winter solstice. The traditional method of preparing this South American drink requires chewing corn as the means of introducing the amylase enzyme ptyalin, which is present in saliva, thus setting in motion the fermentation.

overnight to ferment. Once fermented, it is boiled a second time in order to concentrate its liquids, to which is added starter from a previous batch. The liquid ferments a third time before it is ready to drink. The resulting brew is dark brown in hue and bittersweet in taste, and its alcohol content by volume hovers around 3 per cent.[4]

Every African locality boasts a signature fermented alcoholic drink. Beer anchors communal life, aiding in ceremonies, reaffirming customs and making occasions more festive by promoting good humour, relaxation and nourishment. To know that this is so we need only look to the fact that one-eighth to one-third of grain crops in Africa are consumed as beer.[5]

Scholars have speculated that, although the advent of beer may have owed to a search on humankind's part for easier ways of making bread, beer quickly took precedence over other foods. Recent findings suggest that beer may even pre-date bread. Researchers from the University of Copenhagen in 2018 unearthed fireplaces in northeastern Jordan. The fireplaces, which they estimated to be 14,200 to 14,400 years old, held breadcrumbs that dated to a time before that of grain cultivation, which appeared in history some 4,000 years later. The fireplace owners would therefore have had to wild-harvest any grain they used. Because the difficulty of the task would have discouraged the use of grain in bread merely for eating, the Danish researchers concluded that the crumbs came from loaves baked with the intention of fermenting them with water into alcohol.[6] The findings further suggest that the region's preagricultural inhabitants appeared to have judged a nice buzz ampler reward for the trouble of gathering wild grain than mere nourishment. (Another recent excavation in Haifa, Israel, unearthed a brewery some 13,000 years old.[7])

Knowledge of beer and its heady rewards travelled with nomadic peoples in their wanderings and came to settle in the cities of Mesopotamian civilization. Egyptians, Sumerians and Babylonians all baked loaves of malted barley and wheat. These loaves were covered with water to form a mash, which they placed in an earthen vessel to ferment. And they all kept a portion of the mash in reserve as a starter for the next batch of loaves. Long repetition of this process cemented humankind's relationship with the yeast *Saccharomyces cerevisiae*, and all sorts of attendant customs and observances grew up as a result.

Ancient Mesopotamian art offers an indication that beer drinking took place as a social activity much as it does today. Seals of the period depict human figures from whose mouths project straws into communal vessels.[8] The straws suggest a beer that is unfiltered and filled with sediment. Emmer, barley, spelt and any number of other grains lent themselves to brewing the dark, cloudy stuff, though spelt alone went into premium beer and barley alone into beer of the lowest quality.[9] Whatever the grain or grains, beer

Sumerian cuneiform tablet recording receipt of an allocation of beer. The beverage has its roots in deepest antiquity, its advent perhaps even pre-dating that of bread.

often contained various spices. Some drinkers watered down their aromatic brews; others tippled them at full strength. Pungent and sour, 'small' and refreshing, mixed with wine and honey, served straight up – ancient beer came in an impressive array of choices.

The miracle of alcohol and its powers over humankind naturally attracted the interest of the powerful. Various deities oversaw the production of beer. Because she supervised Sumerians as they brewed, Ninkasi earned the epithet 'the Lady who fills the mouth'. Residing on the fictional Mount Sâbu ('the mount of the taverner'), she spawned nine children, each of whom she named after an alcoholic drink and its signature intoxicating effect. One went by 'the boaster'; another, 'the brawler'. As one might expect of a patroness of booze, Ninkasi inspired great devotion. 'You are the one who handles the dough with a big shovel,' reads a hymn to her from 1800 BCE or thereabouts; 'you are the one who spreads the

Relief depicting the Egyptian god Bes. Like Hathor and other of his peer deities, Bes loved the beer that his worshippers discovered, and he demanded it in tribute for his protection of women on the verge of childbirth.

cooked mash on large reed mats.' Subsequent verses detail further steps in the beer-brewing process before ending with a note of praise on the goddess's fittingly abundant generosity. 'Ninkasi, you are the one who pours out the filtered beer of the collector vat,' it reads: 'it is [like] the onrush of Tigris and Euphrates.'[10]

Whereas Ninkasi played a role in beer brewing, other deities of the era contented themselves with enjoying the final product. Indeed, beer could win their favour, or at least blunt their wrath. 'In honour of the goddess, beer, red with Nubian ochre, is poured in these days of the Feast of the Valley,' reads an inscription on the Egyptian deity Mut's gate at Karnak, 'so that, having been different from the usual aspect of beer, it would appease the anger in her heart.'[11] The goddess Hathor likewise demanded beer – vast quantities of it, in fact – as did Bes, a dwarfish long-tongued god who watched over pregnant women. Images on scarabs depict him in the act of quaffing from a large vessel. The gods' earthly representatives in the ancient Near East exacted their share of beer as well. Jars of it were tendered to Babylonian priests for the performance of certain rites. And many temples in Egypt had their own breweries.

Though undoubtedly popular, beer took a back seat to wine among the elites of ancient Near Eastern societies. The earliest evidence of winemaking in the region appeared at two sites in present-day Iran's Zagros Mountains.[12] The evidence came in the form of a yellowish residue found in six clay jars, each of which could hold 9.5 litres (2.5 U.S. gallons). The residue turned out to be the remains of grape juice and resin. Archaeologists took this as proof that as early as 8,000 years ago peoples of the region between the Black Sea and the Caspian Sea drank a wine that reportedly tasted much like Greek retsina.

As with beer, the art of making wine spread far and wide. All along the Nile and throughout the ancient Near East, great kings sponsored systems for growing and pressing grapes that grew in sophistication as they matured.[13] And also as with beer, wine became associated with the divine. A miraculous vineyard appears in the Sumerian *Epic of Gilgamesh*. Its vines, which represent the tree of life, produce fruit whose juice imparts immortality. It is tended by Siduri, the divine tavern keeper. Later Babylonians expressed their appreciation for the sacredness of wine. On the slopes of their ziggurats – terraced pyramidal towers that housed religious practices – they planted grapes and other fruit.[14]

Divinity made wine a fitting drink for an easy transition to the afterlife. In the tomb of Scorpion 1, a pre-dynastic king of Upper Egypt who died around 3150 BCE, were found jars containing grape seeds and the residue of terebinth resin sealant. These remnants suggest that the jars once held wine. Some jars contained figs, added possibly for enhancing the wine's flavour or boosting its yeast content. In others were found such medicinal herbs as lemon balm, coriander, mint and sage. All told, the tomb contained seven hundred jars in three rooms – capacity enough for 4,000 litres (about 1,057 U.S. gallons) of wine.[15] Wine, it seems, was an essential element of the funeral rite. Rich Egyptians washed in wine when they found themselves *in extremis*. By 5000 BCE burial with wine from the Nile Delta's five most prestigious grape-growing regions became elite custom. Slaves who built the pyramids and performed all socially necessary labour, meanwhile, had to content themselves with beer as a final send-off.

The Greeks similarly attached great cultural importance to wine. In the *Iliad*, Homer – or the collection of anonymous bards who have since come under that name – presents it as a national beverage. Among the many other details in the famous description of Achilles' shield appears an active vineyard.[16] Greeks saw wine as pure, hot and manly. For these reasons it appealed to rich and poor alike.

Beer, on the other hand, they regarded as corrupted, cold and, perhaps worst of all, effeminate. The physician Dioscorides claimed that beer caused elephantiasis;[17] the philosopher Aristotle, stupefaction.[18] There circulated the belief that beer was born from rot. As such, it would cause anyone who drank it to rot. A taste for beer thus offered itself as a handy way of identifying individuals as 'other'. Beer was the drink of Thracians, Phrygians, Egyptians – of foreigners, in short.

The fact that Greeks staked their identity on wine certainly induced them to improve the beverage any way they could. Grapes harvested early in the season retained their acidity, the Greeks found, and drying them on mats preserved their sweetness.[19] The wine itself Greeks diluted, because to their minds only barbarians would drink it straight. And they embellished wine with ingredients that today would come across as unusual. 'Wine is sweet when sea-water is poured into it,' claimed the Greek rhetorician Athenaeus. Greeks perfumed their wine as well. 'And if I tipple, I drink my wine with snow / And a dash o' the finest scent Egyptians know,' wrote the comic poet Dexicrates.[20] Invention often became quite wild, the additives such as to seem to make for an unpalatable drink. 'In Greece,' wrote Pliny the Elder, 'they enliven the smoothness of their wines with potter's earth or marble dust.'[21] The poor, on the other hand, seldom enjoyed such licence. For them, wine was catch as catch can. Sometimes high, sometimes low, its quality varied according to the vagaries of production and elite tastes. The poor most often had to content themselves with the lees of whatever vintage the rich had consumed.

The class distinctions imposed by wine relaxed somewhat with the festivities of Dionysus. Thickly bearded and bearing a fennel staff topped with a pine cone, the wine god arrived from the East to deliver his devotees into transports of unreason. (A later incarnation finds him more androgynous in appearance, having thick curls, pale skin and no beard.) The Bacchae, as his adherents came to be called, engaged in the rites of his festival, namely, frenzied dancing and chaotic behaviour. Historian Edward Hyams describes the rites as having had 'the tenor and madness of a really bad drunk-in-charge-of-car case'. Though they were 'full of laughter', he continues, they were of 'a terrible sound' and 'wild play'.[22] The god of fertility, political protest and the unknown and unseen as well as wine, Dionysus presided over a cult that swept Europe, its themes of intoxication and ecstatic abandon no doubt hugely appealing.

As Roman influence overtook Greek, wine grew in popularity. The Etruscans, a people descended from Minoan or Mycenaean migrants, introduced the vine to northern Italy, where they had been growing it since their contact with the Phoenicians in 800 BCE. The Hellenic cities to the south also contributed to wine production. Whatever its origins in Italy, its development advanced considerably under the Romans, whose expertise owed to having to learn to grow grapes in different climates. The longer ripening and later harvesting of grapes, for example, were probably their

An amphora bearing an image of Dionysus. Originally an exotic god imported from the East, Dionysus eventually found a home in the spiritual and cultural life of Greece.

invention. 'Be the first to dig the land, the first to wheel off the prunings,' counsels the poet Virgil in his *Georgics*: 'For the bonfire, the first to bring your vine-poles under cover; / But the last to gather the vintage.'[23] Romans also made use of the wine press more regularly than the Greeks. In fact, they relied on technology generally, mechanizing winemaking to an unprecedented extent. In all but the most rural reaches of their empire, where winemakers continued to press grapes with heavy stones and wicker baskets, the screw press saw use. It was employed in Gaul, in the Rhineland and in such important present-day wine regions as Champagne and Burgundy.[24]

Other techniques varied by region. In the northern and western reaches of their empire Romans fermented the must – that is, the freshly crushed fruit, seeds and stems combined – in stone tanks or wooden barrels. In the south they more often used large clay jars called *dolia*.[25] Because they had at their disposal no sulphur, an effective inhibitor of bad bacterial growth with which to control fermentation, vessels would often explode in hot weather. To avoid such an unhappy event Cato the Elder, who wrote extensively on agriculture, recommended that winemakers bury the vessels in the ground or submerge them in ponds for thirty days. Wine thus treated would 'stay sweet for the whole year', he claimed.[26]

The Romans became so skilled in wine that they created plenty of it. A steady supply meant that members of all classes had access to the stuff. Slaves who worked the vineyards owned by the rich eased the pangs of their labours with it. And it lubricated the so-called 'bread and circuses', a social policy of free food and spectacles that sought to distract the thronging urban masses into sustained, if uneasy, complacency. A gladiatorial match, for example, might see tens of thousands of amphorae be handed out to attendees. At one such event Cleopatra's son Ptolemy Philadelphus gave out a reported 20,000 gallons of wine, which came delivered in a giant panther-skin bag.[27]

Image of King Zhou of the late Shang Dynasty. The very picture of decadence, Zhou ordered the construction of a pool, which he then ordered to be filled with wine. This he did to impress his concubine. The pool saw much use, as Zhou ordered unclothed men and women to disport themselves in and around it.

The insight that wine presented a useful sociopolitical lubricant for advancing state ends had occurred to the ancient Chinese millennia before it had to elite Romans. In China the formative winemaking period began with the Neolithic early Yangshao culture (5000–3000 BCE) and continued into the Xia Dynasty (2070–1600 BCE), with subsequent improvements occurring between the Xia and Zhou Dynasties (1046–256 BCE). Made from millet, sorghum, rice and various fruits, this early wine became of great interest to state officials, just as it had in ancient Egypt and Mesopotamia. Special bureaus managed winemaking, and there circulated no small amount of advice on how to produce the best vintages.[28]

Winemakers developed an exacting process for making a sound ferment – the 'backbone of the wine', as one saying went – methods of which appeared in *The Book of Rites*, a classic Confucian work of the late Zhou Dynasty. It directs winemakers to use only ripe grain and spotless implements and vessels, add their ferment at the right moment, boil only clean water at a proper temperature for the right amount of time, and pour the final product only into containers of high-quality ceramic.[29]

Better winemaking techniques over time made for better wine. And as wine improved in quality, it began to appeal to 'the quality'. Aristocrats of the Shang Dynasty (1600–1046 BCE) held drinking parties. In the dynasty's final years King Zhou, a renowned sensualist, had a pool built that he ordered to be filled with wine. (He also had constructed for his pleasure a forest of meat.) He commanded men and women to swim in it naked and to chase one another around it. King Zhou's wine-pool orgies exemplified the decadence that would come to topple the dynasty and prompt the creation of China's first anti-wine regulations.[30]

\* \* \*

A seemingly unassuming fermented drink, wine could help to bring down ruling families, as it had ancient China's Zhou Dynasty, and even entire empires. When Rome finally fell in 456 CE, wine tainted with lead may have played a part, as some scholars suspect, by causing various physical and cognitive debilities among the elite. Whatever the role of wine, tainted or otherwise, in the event, its place in the succeeding order was secure. Ownership of Roman vineyards throughout the empire transferred to the conquering barbarians of northern Europe, who, though customarily beer drinkers, came to learn the value of the grape. Indeed, they came to cherish it, meting out severe penalties to whomever should damage vines. The ninth-century monarch of the Iberian kingdom of Asturias, King Ordoño I, placed the vineyards near

Coimbra (located in present-day west-central Portugal) under the protection of a monastic order.

Under the mantle of monastic protection came beer, as well. Christian monks saw alcohol as recalling the divine, a common association with spirits perhaps informing the perception. (Spirits such as brandy and vodka would not be consumed for pleasure until the sixteenth century, when improvements in distilling and flavour enhancers made them more palatable.) They not only preserved Roman winemaking traditions, but adopted and refined the beer-brewing ways of the barbarian conquerors, growing spelt, wheat, oats, rye and barley, some of which they used for ale. In time ale became an important source of income and influence for orders that brewed it. Word of an exceptional ale might circulate by way of pilgrims and travelling merchants who had lodged at a cloister. Churches used ale as a way of drawing festival attendees and hosting guild events; guild members would more probably choose a venue that they knew to hold abundant stores of the stuff.[31]

In the use of alcohol as a means of wielding power, amassing wealth and gaining influence, the medieval Church recalled the precedent set by the states of the ancient Near and Far East as well as the later Greek and Roman. Yet it was only a matter of time before states in the West, resurgent at the close of the Dark Ages (476–800), began to seek such means for their own ends. European towns grew in population, size and diversity of trade. Breweries, taverns and inns sprang up – usually near sources of water. (And not just any water would do. Water with too much lime in it affected fermentation; water with too much iron, clarity.)

Along with any constraints imposed on makers and sellers of beer by nature came those imposed on them by government. In England William the Conqueror (c. 1028–1087) appointed for the City of London four 'ale-conners' and tasked them with assuring that the ale sold by ale houses was fit for consumption. Taverners knew an ale-conner by his leather breeches, at once part of his

A monk brewing beer. The medieval Christian Church stood with the civilizations of the ancient Near East and Egypt in its recognition of the tremendous power inherent in beer. Beer brewed by monastic orders conformed to exacting standards, which ensured that its quality would be high enough to draw parishioners and townsfolk to fairs and other fundraising endeavours.

uniform and the tool of his trade. He went about his inspection by wetting a settle with some beer. He would then sit in the puddle for thirty minutes or so. If, on rising, his breeches did not stick he would deem the beer fit for sale. (Any stickiness would have betrayed the presence of residual sugars in the beer, a sure sign of an incomplete ferment.[32]) Other regulations began to appear on the books in England and on the Continent in the centuries that followed. Henry V (1387–1422) added an element of solemnity to ale-conning with an oath of office. And in 1551 England and Wales began to require licences of alehouse proprietors. The *Reinheitsgebot* issued by Duke William VI of Bavaria in 1516 names water, barley and hops as the only allowable ingredients for beer. It has remained in force to this day.

Behind regulations and the concern for purity lay a commercial impulse. Mercantile sorts saw beer as a potentially lucrative export. The first documentation of the export of English ale comes from an account of Thomas à Becket's visit to France in 1158. His train to Paris included two chariots laden with iron-bound barrels of ale brewed, as Becket's clerk records, 'from choice fat grain', brought as 'a gift for the French'. On sampling it, its recipients 'wondered at such an invention', which they judged 'a drink most whole-some, clear of all dregs, rivalling wine in colour, and surpassing it in savour'.[33]

For all its wholesomeness and surpassing savour, English ale did not keep well. Becket and his retinue probably had to hurry if they wished to get anything drinkable to their Parisian hosts. Brewers of the time could only make ale transportable by fermenting it until its alcohol content became quite high. A second option, however, later arrived in the form of hops. Added to a barley wort after mashing and prior to yeast activation, its dried blossoms release lupulone and humulone, two resins that act as preservatives.[34] A well-preserved beer had hops in it; a delicate ale had none.

And well-preserved stood the brewery trade into the bargain. Hops helped it to endure – indeed, thrive. On brewery grounds grew hops gardens, especially in Flanders, northern and eastern France and Bavaria, all regions where the climate proved suitable. (The English preferred sweeter ales and therefore did not regularly hop beer until 1700.) The hops from these gardens let breweries move their beer to markets that had theretofore remained out of reach.[35]

In doing so, hops transformed a perishable domestic beverage into the perfect global commodity. Beer enjoyed enduring popularity throughout Europe for its intoxicating effects, its consequent constant market demand and its amenability to regulation and taxation. It seemed a dream come true for maker, merchant and sovereign alike, the last seeing it as an ideal vehicle for various duties, taxes and fees that could fill his state's coffers. For this reason the law played a greater role in brewing than it did in almost any other industry in Europe.[36] Assessors measured beer, weighed it, quantified it whatever its vessel, and appraised its qualities – strength, clarity and so on. And all the while rulers watched closely, enamoured with this most lucrative ferment.

But some did more than watch. Indeed, not a few took measures to ensure their breweries could compete with the best. These measures became even more important during the fourteenth century, when rivalry grew quite fierce among nations that exported beer.

In the Netherlands, for example, hopped beers from member towns of the Hanseatic League, a confederation of guilds and market towns along the north coast of Germany, had crowded out local offerings. To survive, Dutch brewers found themselves forced to change the way they produced beer. Their sovereigns, understanding the importance of beer to the economy, lent a hand. In the latter half of the fourteenth century, the Counts of Holland launched a policy of economic development. Under their direction, drainage projects recovered land for growing the cereal grains essential to brewing, and rights to settlement granted to towns allowed them to set up breweries and attendant trades. They also imposed tariffs on foreign beer and grain, and, in some districts, prohibited the import of German beer altogether.[37] The policies had the effect of increasing Dutch beer production over the two centuries that followed. And with more beer came more government regulation.

Yet Dutch brewers adapted the use of hops to the new economic, social and legislative environment to great effect. Traditional Dutch beer recipes depended on gruit, a mixture of herbs that

After D. Teniers the Younger, *Two Dutch Topers Clasping a Beer Jug and Smoking,*
c. 1831, mezzotint. With use of hops in brewing, Holland became a beer-exporting
powerhouse. And its domestic consumption of the stuff was prodigious as
well. Variety, sensible taxation and regulations combined to sustain the brewing
industry, and Dutch society prospered as no other early modern European
nation had before.

might have contained sweet gale, mugwort, yarrow, ground ivy,
horehound and heather. Sometimes there also appeared juniper
berries, ginger, caraway seed, aniseed, nutmeg and cinnamon. Gruit
occasionally even had hops in it, albeit in amounts insufficient for
preserving beer for export. Exchanging hops for gruit, along with
changes to the brewing process, enabled the Dutch to brew beer
that matched, if not surpassed, German beer in quality.

The long-term strategic investment paid off. The period saw brewing make its greatest financial contribution to the Dutch economy, knock-on benefits reaching such related trades as shipping and cooperage.[38] Municipalities gained as well. The city of Amsterdam, for example, came to rely on the excise tax on wine, beer and grain as its single greatest source of revenue – some 70 per cent by 1552. The newly vibrant economic life of the early modern Netherlands buoyed political and social life along with it.[39]

Of course, any society reliant on taxes will have its tax-exempt members. Nobles paid no drink-related excise; nor did monks, beguines or shipbuilders. This privilege they shared with lepers.[40]

Those who did have to pay seem not to have minded, the effects of the item taxed no doubt doing something to ease the pain of any such burden. The Dutch established a reputation as prodigious drinkers, and it preceded them. Elizabethan poet Thomas Nashe complained about a 'superfluity in drink' among his countrymen, a problem he blamed on foreign influence consequent upon Britain's political involvement in the Low Countries. Indeed, only water surpassed beer as the most common drink in Holland. Estimates put per capita beer consumption in the fifteenth and sixteenth centuries at some 400 litres a year. Adults drank as much as 4 litres a day on average, with skilled workers in the various industries tending to knock back even more.[41] And beer flowed as cheaply as it did freely, despite the taxes on it. A tavern would charge half a *stuiver* – roughly u.s.$1.19 or £0.91 in today's money – for a tankard of it in the 1650s.[42]

Aside from its obvious appeal as an intoxicant, beer became so beloved by the Dutch because it admitted of variety, falling roughly into three categories: expensive and high-quality, cheap and thin, and somewhere in between.[43] Beer of the first category, if not exported, had herbs added to it for sale to the wealthy. The breweries of Delft, Haarlem and Amersfoort established a reputation for particularly strong brews. Their beer became something of a status symbol, and they did what they could to preserve an aura of exclusivity. Beer of the second category usually ended up as table beer; beer of the third, general purpose. Strength and perceived value depended on whether the beer came from the first, second, third or even fourth mashing. Sometimes herbs and spices in beer added flavour for the refined palates of the rich, and sometimes they imparted properties for promoting health and wellness. The town of Dordrecht, for example, produced an especially esteemed medicinal beer.[44] *Kuit*, an un-hopped ale rich in oats, became exceedingly popular. Those who favoured heavy brews drank *dickenbier* and *swarer poortersbier*. *Scharbier* was weak, its appeal resting on its purity rather than any heady effects. Its weakness exempted it from taxes. Similarly untaxed and weaker still was *scheepsbier*, or ship's beer.[45]

Such variety compelled town and city governments to issue legislation governing accuracy in beer's production and labelling. The legislation identified and enforced distinctions according to a beer's additives and colour. This latter distinction in turn depended on the type of malt used and the time of year of brewing, as well as a beer's strength, intended customer and place of origin. The legislation further mandated the use of certain recipes and quantities of grain – usually oats, wheat, rye and, the cheapest, barley. And it prescribed the time that newly brewed beer was to remain warehoused in order to ensure proper fermentation.[46]

The new laws largely failed, however, because licence taken behind the scenes at breweries, whether innocent or subversive, made any uniform standards all but impossible to enforce. A brewer might call his offering *dickenbier*, say, but what he brought to market would have deviated from a legislated recipe to such an extent as to have become a novel beer.[47] In an age before mass communications, getting brewers to act in concert proved a tall order.

What had required no legislation to preserve it was brewing itself, which had remained largely unchanged since the days of the Egyptian pharaohs. Understanding of that which occurred in brewing – the fermentation process – had changed, however, growing in sophistication and detail. Though the Dutch knew of both top- and bottom-fermenting yeast, historical evidence suggests that they preferred beer made from the former. (They may nevertheless have also used slow-acting bottom-fermenting yeast for winter brews.) Yeast inoculation varied from brewer to

Barley, from a 19th-century German textbook. Of the various grains that went into beer, all of which were strictly mandated under Dutch law, barley was the least expensive. It therefore found its way into a wide variety of beers in the Netherlands.

brewer. Some added beer from a previous batch to start the process. Others tossed bread into the mash. Still others simply left their equipment uncleaned as a way of preserving the residues of earlier batches. This last technique sometimes left batches exposed to contamination by unwanted yeasts. Yet by the fifteenth century, brewers increasingly came to keep their yeast cultures safe from contamination in clean vessels. They would add this uncontaminated yeast once they had poured the wort into fermenting troughs. To determine that the wort had fermented thoroughly, they would bring a lit candle near it. If the candle went out they knew that it had, because the carbon dioxide issuing from it had reached a level high enough to starve a flame.[48]

The fifteenth, sixteenth and seventeenth centuries saw few, if any, changes made to the process of brewing in the Netherlands. Equipment essential to the brewing trade included tuns (large casks) for mashing, kettles for boiling wort and water, cooling troughs, fermenting troughs and barrels, and various hand tools – shovels for stoking and moving grain, rakes, and paddles for stirring. Primary fermentation of a bottom-fermenting beer took place in deep troughs over ten to twelve days. Following this, a secondary fermentation took place in casks. Brewers left some space in the casks, which they sealed for storage in a place into which cooling breezes could reach. Fermentation of a top-fermenting ale took place over three days in a cask.[49] For clarifying beer, top- or bottom-fermented, brewers might use pig's or ox's feet, clean sand or lime, ground oak bark or dried fish bladders, also known as isinglass.[50] This last agent remains in use today.

In beer the Dutch found an export that would help them amass the riches they would devote to funding an empire. Soon other countries came to join the Netherlands in the beer trade once they had managed to improve their brewing. In 1553 Bavaria's Duke Albrecht v outlawed the activity during summer months; hot weather affected yeast such that it produced beer that was too

*The Vintagers, After a Miniature of the 'Dialogues de Saint Gregoire', c.* 13th century. Among the various fermented beverages, wine has best resisted various attempts at standardization and industrial production. The duties and demands of its making root it stubbornly in long tradition. Best practices have thus remained largely unaltered since the Middle Ages, and, indeed, classical antiquity.

unpleasantly scented and flavoured to sell. He decreed a brewing season that ran from St Michael's Day (29 September) to St George's Day (23 April).[51] Bottom-fermenting yeast fared well in the cooler weather, producing beers that were light in colour and flavourful. Unsurprisingly, they proved popular. This popularity soon translated to Bohemia, where a citizen-owned brewery in the city of Plzeň – or Pilsen, as German speakers knew it – had developed a beer of a lovely pale colour and delicate yet slightly bitter taste. The winning combination of flavour and appearance owed to the brewery's water, which was soft and contained few impurities.[52]

There was just one problem. The yeast used in the brewery could behave unpredictably, producing the odd sour batch. It seemed that the softest water in the world could do little to prevent such spoilage.

And what of wine? Its inextricable connection to place also made it difficult to standardize and commodify. So much depended on its terroir – the local bedrock, soil, water, microclimate and many other elements – that for all but the cheapest varieties the production process tended to defy mechanization. And as with beer, microorganisms could spoil the product of an entire vintage, much to the dismay of vintners.

But it was not for a lack of trying. As we will learn in the chapter to follow, the efforts of that venerable grandee of microbiology, Louis Pasteur, led to a quality-assurance breakthrough in winemaking, mostly as concerned preventing spoilage. Yet other individuals would translate the substance of Pasteur's breakthrough to beer, and the results would be far-reaching and transformative.

# 2 'Un Grand Progrès': *The Industrialization of Fermented Drink*

Brewing the best way hard money to win is:
Guinness makes porter, and porter makes guineas.
– R. E. Egerton-Warburton, 'On Visiting the Great
Dublin Brewery'[1]

IN NINETEENTH-CENTURY France bad wine was a big problem. The French Revolution had liberated vineyards from aristocrats, who tended to prize quality over quantity, and put them under the ownership of peasants, who ramped up production to a point where wine came to rival grain as a major commodity. Fields became vineyards and by 1850 grapevines occupied 2 million hectares of French soil. And a good thing, too: wine had become immensely popular among all classes. French peasants, soldiers and factory workers all drank wine when they could, and every bourgeois tried to keep a well-stocked cellar. But wine produced on a mass scale, though valiantly attempted, had yet to be perfected: season after season saw massive losses from disease and other blights.[2]

To vintners these wine diseases seemed to work an infernal magic. A seemingly fine white wine turned greasy; a red wine, bitter. Warm weather might birth silky waves of filamentous material that resembled clouds in both red and white wine. The wines of the Loire Valley and Orléans lost their limpidity and turned flat, flavourless and viscous.[3] A barrel bulging from the diseased wine within it was said to have 'the pushes'. Worst of all, disease could kill a wine's taste. One major vintner in Montpellier faced bankruptcy when his wine, which he thought first rate and advertised as such, was suspected of having been watered down, so insipid had disease made it. Sales of it tanked and with them his fortunes.

This was unhappy enough when wine was confined to French tables, but once France entered a free-trade agreement with Great Britain in 1860, diseased wine went from secret shame to open embarrassment.[4] Exported stuff often turned sour and bitter – if it managed to avoid becoming so gelatinous as to prevent decanting. Unimpressed, the British stopped buying French wine. 'The reason for this is rather simple,' one wholesale merchant explained. 'In the beginning we eagerly greeted the arrival of these wines, but we soon made the sad experience that this trade caused great losses and endless trouble because of the diseases to which they are subject.'[5]

Enter Louis Pasteur, a servant as faithful to scientific enquiry as he was to the state. In 1863 Emperor Napoleon III asked him to investigate the cause of wine disease. Pasteur was certainly the right man for the job. He had already disproved the doctrine of spontaneous generation, which posited that microorganisms can spring from non-living matter, and he was well on his way to understanding the complexities of fermentation. In 1860 he published the impressive 'Mémoire sur la fermentation alcoolique', which contained a careful account of the history of the subject as well as detailed descriptions of his experiments. In it he refuted the prevailing theory that alcohol resulted from chemical fermentation, and that, rather than a catalyst of this process, yeast was simply a by-product. Pasteur showed that one medium could give rise to different ferments depending on the microorganisms introduced.

Louis Pasteur, the towering figure of 19th-century microbiology whose studies led to new understanding of fermentation, bacterial infection and disease prevention.

Yeast produced one kind of ferment, lactic acid bacteria another.[6] His results suggested, then, that one could control the quality of a ferment by controlling the kind of microorganism present in it.

Pasteur's intervention proved timely, as no such control was anywhere evident in French winemaking. The pioneering micro-biologist opined that, owing to rampant disease, 'there may not be a single winery in France, whether rich or poor, where some portions of the wine have not suffered greater or lesser alteration.'[7]

To conduct his experiments Pasteur travelled to his home town of Arbois. Famous for rosy and tawny wines, Arbois lay at the heart of the Jura wine-producing region. There a young Pasteur had romped among vineyards.[8] Now with three of his students he took over the back room of a local café, setting up his microscope,

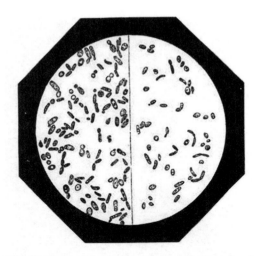

Reproduction of a drawing made by Pasteur of microorganisms he observed in wine. He concluded that they caused wine to spoil, become bitter or turn otherwise undrinkable.

incubator, tubules, tube holders, gas jets and other instruments important to his experiments. Behind the counter were samples of wines from the surrounding regions.[9] Ever thorough, Pasteur also purchased a vineyard on Arbois' outskirts. There he could observe every stage of winemaking, from picking to racking.

Pasteur's own presence in the wine-growing region did not go unobserved. Unhappy with the quality of their wine, vintners from the most prestigious vineyards sent samples to him. Pasteur examined them through his microscope and saw the close, round clusters of bacteria that turned even the finest vintage greasy and ropey.

The challenge went from discovering the wine-spoiling microbes to eradicating them. Chemicals proved difficult to work with because they produced unreliable and often unpalatable results. Pasteur decided to try heat-treating a bacterium that caused French wines to taste bitter. He took 25 bottles of the best wines from Burgundy, Beaune and Pommard, all from different years (1858, 1862 and 1863), and let them stand for 48 hours to allow any particles present to settle. He then siphoned off the wine in such a way as to leave the sediment undisturbed. When only 1 cubic centimetre remained in each bottle, he shook up the contents and examined the residue with a microscope. The wine itself had not yet become bitter, but Pasteur knew it was simply a matter of time. If allowed to mature the filaments would work their characteristic effect.[10]

Pasteur then heated a bottle of each regional wine to 60°c (140°F). He cooled them and laid them alongside unheated bottles in a cellar whose temperature hovered between 13 and 17°c (55.4 and 62.6°F), depending on the season. Every fifteen days he held the bottles up to the light to check for the formation of filaments. He found that in less than six weeks a floating deposit formed in all the unheated bottles, the wines bottled in 1863 containing the most. In the heated bottles, on the other hand, not a single deposit appeared.[11] To celebrate this breakthrough Pasteur drank any wine he discovered to be free of filaments.

Pasteur's experiments challenged prevailing theories of fermentation. To brewers and vintners, making alcoholic drinks was more art than science. A batch that turned out well spoke of the maker's skill. More scientifically minded folk sought a more objective explanation for the process. Citing experimental results that were dubious yet popular, they came to conceive of fermentation as a chemical reaction.

This conception, however, had emerged only recently. Until the end of the eighteenth century, fermentation's mechanism remained largely a mystery, though its effects had been acknowledged and duly taxonomized. Early observers had made note of the acetic fermentation of vinegar, the lactic fermentation of soured milk and even a putrid fermentation, this last marked by the fetid smell that came from spoiled meat, rotten eggs and other decomposing organic matter.[12] But they did not know why exactly apple juice turned to vinegar or raw milk to bonny clabber.

The few theories that emerged were mechanistic or chemical in nature. The seventeenth-century French philosopher and mathematician René Descartes thought the bubbling in a vat of beer or wine owed to forces that mixed with and displaced one another. The pioneering eighteenth-century French chemist Antoine Laurent Lavoisier followed suit and moreover marshalled mathematics in support. He explained fermentation as expressive of a balanced equation and algebraic formulation wherein if one places sugar on one pan of a scale, it is balanced after fermentation by the sum of the weight of the carbonic acid it has yielded and of the alcohol it has formed.[13] Air and motion encouraged fermentation because they induced movement; which was why, according to chemists, grapes must be crushed, dough kneaded and beer wort mashed.

Perhaps surprisingly, there also prevailed a belief that fermentation proceeded by way of putrefaction rather than reproduction.[14] Though apparently lively, an effervescing vat of wine or beer evidenced death, decomposition. The yeast aided beer brewing in its destruction, which occurred in the chemical transformation that was the fermenting wort. The same process was imputed to wine that had been infused with vinegar. Through the several variations of the prevailing theory remained one immutable tenet: fermentation was a chemical rather than a biological phenomenon. Anyone who claimed otherwise risked being considered wrong-headed, if not delusional.

But Pasteur could not deny what his experiments had revealed: namely, that fermentation had a biological cause.

His findings set him at odds with Justus von Liebig, the greatest champion of the chemical-fermentation theory. Chair of chemistry at the University of Munich, member of the Académie des sciences, Britain's Royal Society and just about every important learned organization in Europe and America, and a baron to boot, Liebig had lived through the worldwide famine of 1816, the so-called 'year without a summer', an experience that left him with a marked practicality of purpose. He took an interest in chemistry, which at the time was kissing cousin to alchemy and other mystic arts.

Liebig sought to free the young science from this association and win for it proper respect. As his lean early years had taught him, turning it to solving social and industrial problems was the way to do so. He developed artificial meat and milk extracts as well as bouillon cubes that fed the Prussian army during its war with France of 1870.[15] He also developed fertilizers and advanced important theories of nutrition. Indeed, his contribution proved so transformative and lasting that the famines of his childhood came to represent the last great natural subsistence crisis in the Western world. (There would, alas, be many more man-made crises.) Despite his great learning, however, he clung to the theories of alcoholic fermentation that Pasteur had come to regard as quite exploded.

Liebig's devotion to outmoded theories told most in the German vinegar industry, which he helped to oversee. In Liebig's time the traditional 'beechwood shavings method' for making vinegar dominated. In it makers dripped wine or beer onto a bed of beechwood shavings piled in a large barrel. Holes in the barrel provided air, and makers deemed the vinegar ready when it had passed through the wood.[16] Liebig believed the process owed to the shavings, which acted like dry rot, and to the exposure of alcohol to the action of oxygen in the atmosphere: one-third of the quantity of hydrogen contained in the liquid is withdrawn, and aldehyde forms as a result. The aldehyde in turn combines with oxygen and converts to acetic acid. The shavings acted as porous bodies, and the vinegar was formed by a direct oxidation, the wood's porosity being the sole agent. The process of vinegar formation was one of partial combustion, Liebig believed; it had nothing to do with biological phenomena.[17]

Pasteur doubted Liebig's theory. In 1861 he visited vinegar factories in Orléans to observe vinegar-making for himself and

Justus von Liebig, the pioneering German scientist who advanced the field of chemistry despite his adherence to outmoded theories, one of which was his belief that putrefaction rather than reproduction explained the action of fermentation.

determine whether it needed improvement. Tending to contaminate the vinegar was a type of nematode known as an eelworm, which manufacturers believed important to the process. Pasteur knew better. Observing that the vinegar barrels were poorly filtered, he surmised that such conditions fostered the growth of undesirable organisms to the detriment of desirable ones. The 'mother of vinegar' – the gelatinous mass of beneficial organisms that formed on the liquid's surface – alone made for successful ferments. Allow the mother to remain exposed and the process continued; plunge it below the liquid's surface and it ceased.[18] Confident in his conclusions, Pasteur took out a patent that presented *Mycoderma aceti*, the bacteria that form a 'mother', as the sole cause of wine's becoming vinegar.[19]

Pasteur shared with Liebig his finding that beechwood shavings aid vinegar-making because they harbour the *M. aceti* organisms that themselves alone do the work. The elder chemist responded with scepticism, prompting Pasteur to ask him to have a look for himself by examining the shavings under a microscope. For good measure Pasteur also asked Liebig to send some shavings to the Académie, whose members would decide the issue once and for all.

Liebig never responded. All the better, Pasteur reasoned, for such stubborn silence would be to Germany's economic detriment; in light of the losses France had suffered in the Franco-Prussian War, this prospect was a cheery one. The conflict may have humiliated the French on the battlefield, but they could still triumph in industries such as beer brewing and winemaking.

But Pasteur also gained an important insight: microbes could determine the fate of nations. 'When we see beer and wine subjected to deep alterations because they have given refuge to microorganisms invisibly introduced and now swarming within them,' he wrote, 'it is impossible not to be pursued by the thought that similar facts may, *must*, take place in animals.'[20] From 1870 on, Pasteur would apply all that he had learned from his study of fermentation to combating some of the most destructive diseases of the time, from rabies to anthrax. And the food industries that benefited from his findings would continue to perfect methods for mass-producing the fermented foods that had previously been made by traditional means, changing what and how people ate.

*  *  *

In January 1877, Danish brewer Jacob Christian (J. C.) Jacobsen came under the spell of Pasteur's theories. Jacobsen believed that a treatise written by Pasteur on hygiene in beer production held the key to solving a serious problem plaguing his brewery, Carlsberg: batches of beer turned rank and sour. Jacobsen's business ambitions were such that his bottom line could ill absorb such loss to spoilage. He sought to brew beer on an industrial scale to sell to his countrymen and -women, who, like the French, had begun to drink alcoholic beverages in volumes never before seen. Eager to meet this demand, Jacobsen wrote to the University of Copenhagen's Japetus Steenstrup. In his letter he asked whether the good professor knew of someone familiar with Pasteur's techniques. It turned out that Steenstrup did. And that someone was Emil Christian Hansen.

The son of an alcoholic ex-soldier father and laundress mother, Hansen was a restive dreamer who early in life wished to become an actor. When that career path met a dead end he apprenticed to a grocery merchant, only to be dismissed for being too unruly. There followed stints in house painting and, later, portrait painting, rejection from the Academy of Fine Arts ending any future in the latter. He entertained becoming a soldier like his father and enlisted in the army of Italian nationalist general Giuseppe Garibaldi, but he abandoned the idea for that of teaching. Hansen stuck with this for a while, until, inspired by a local botanist and fellow teacher, he decided to take a degree in natural history from the University of Copenhagen. There he developed a lifelong obsession with microorganisms, the pursuit of which he subsidized by writing stories for almanacs and magazines as E. C. Hansen. He would later go on to translate the British naturalist Charles Darwin's *The Voyage of the Beagle* into Danish.[21]

A gold medal won for an essay on the fungi that grow on mammalian manure confirmed to Hansen that he had finally found his calling. He went on to study fermentation physiology at the laboratory of Professor Peter Ludwig Panum. While conducting these studies news of Jacobsen's search for a scientist to study yeast reached him. Hansen decided he would be that scientist, but he first had to complete his doctoral dissertation on the microorganisms found in beer. What he would discover built on Pasteur's work of a few years prior to revolutionize yeast's use in industrial brewing.

For centuries yeast was only slightly less mysterious than bacteria. Though awareness of it was well established – *yeast* comes from the Old English *gist* (sometimes *gyst*), whose Indo-European root *yes-* means 'boil', 'foam' or 'bubble' – as was its use in brewing beer and baking bread, its mechanism remained a mystery. Any expansion of its inclusion in food and drink proceeded by trial and error. In the late seventeenth century Dutch merchant Antonie van Leeuwenhoek first identified a yeast cell. Peering at a drop of beer through a compound microscope of his own making, he observed bodies, some of which were 'quite round'. He also noted that 'others were irregular, and some exceeded the others in size'. He went on to observe that some seemed to consist of 'two, three or four . . . particles joined together', whereas others were 'of six globules [that] formed a complete globule of yeast'.[22]

The discovery that such globules were present in beer certainly signalled progress in understanding. But understanding had yet to arrive at why they were present. As scientists continued to puzzle

Emil Christian Hansen in his laboratory. It was there that many of his important investigations into the nature and behaviour of microorganisms translated to advances in beer brewing on an industrial scale.

over the problem, brewers themselves began to hazard theories. In his 1762 work *The Theory and Practice of Brewing*, British brewer Michael Combrune claimed somewhat perplexingly that 'sensible internal motion of the particles of a mixture, by the continuance of this motion particles are gradually removed from their former situation, and after some visible separation, joined together in a different order and arrangement so as to constitute a new compound.'[23] A process that stretched into eternity, fermentation was, for him, this ceaseless motion. 'That this operation persists even after the liquor becomes fine is evident, for every fretting is a continuance of fermentation,' Combrune concluded. 'It would seem that the more minutely the parts are reduced, the more pungency will appear, and the easier their passage be in the human frame.'[24]

Adding to the perplexity over the need for yeast in making beer was the absence of need for it in making wine, a beverage that appeared to ferment spontaneously. Combrune attempted to explain the difference by positing that in wine fermentation there inhered from the outset heat sufficient for setting in motion the various necessary particles, whereas in beer fermentation exposure to heat in the forms of boiling and kilning removed air from the wort, which therefore needed yeast as a catalyst. Combrune felt it should be added in stages so that 'the air bladders; all bursting at once, should prevent that gradual action which is the aim of nature.'[25] Though his rather abstruse explanation did little to dispel the confusion, it did represent a real attempt to discover why certain foods and beverages needed certain microorganisms for their creation.

As the eighteenth century gave way to the nineteenth these attempts only increased. In his *Practical Treatise on Brewing* of 1805 Richard Shannon wrote that fermentation was 'Nature's way of decomposing and recombining constituents of fermentable substances in presence of sufficient water', a way 'allied to respiration and . . . evidently a low form of combustion'.[26] William

Roberts, meanwhile, offered his hard-nosed appraisal of the state of enquiry. In his *Scottish Ale Brewer*, published in 1847, he wrote of fermentation that 'the mystery in which its principles are involved continues to present an unpenetrated barrier,' before going on to lambast 'those who dogmatically profess to have encompassed this subtle and complicated subject' for having proven 'the extent of their ignorance and presumption' in their theories.[27]

An accurate description of the actions of the agent in the elixir that was beer would not arrive until 1835. In that year French mechanical engineer Charles Cagniard de la Tour monitored, through a microscope, the changes that yeast underwent during fermentation. What he saw led him to proclaim yeast a living organism akin to plants, one that could cause alcoholic fermentation.[28] One influential German scientist, Theodor Schwann, came to a similar conclusion two years later when he demonstrated that alcoholic fermentation was the result of a living mass of yeast. He prepared solutions of cane sugar and introduced to them two kinds of air: heated air that he had isolated, and air that he drew from the surrounding atmosphere.[29] When he introduced the heated air, the solution did not ferment. When he introduced the ambient air, the solution did. Moreover, he witnessed yeast budding and observed 'several cells within one cell', or sporulation.[30] He glimpsed, in short, the biological workings of a microbe responsible for many favourite foods. To this microbe Schwann gave the name *Zuckerpilz* (sugar fungus).[31]

Cagniard de la Tour and Schwann's theories were simply two among many, and they had to contend with those which held fermentation to be solely a chemical process. Swedish count Jöns Jacob Berzelius, called the 'arbiter and dictator of the chemical world' by biochemist Arthur Harden, accepted the role yeast played in fermentation, but considered it, as he wrote, 'no more a living organism than was a precipitate of alumina'.[32] Berzelius considered yeast to be a 'catalytic force' that 'enabled bodies, by their mere

Jöns Jacob Berzelius, who ascended to a position of preeminence in the then-young field of chemistry. He held the opinion that yeast, whose presence had been observed in various fermented food and drink, played the role of catalyst rather than agent in the fermentation process. It was this opinion, which other leading chemists of the day shared, that Pasteur and Hansen would later overturn on the strength of their respective findings.

presence, and not by their affinity, to arouse affinities ordinarily quiescent at the temperature of the experiment, so that the elements of a compound body arrange themselves in some different way, by which a greater degree of electro-chemical neutralisation is attained'.[33] In other words, yeast precipitated the production of alcohol; it did not itself produce alcohol.

Pasteur's foil Justus von Liebig also saw fermentation as solely chemical. He believed that the process brought about the conversion of carbon in sugar to carbon dioxide and alcohol through a charge 'set up by the access of air to the plant juices containing sugar, and which contained all the nitrogen of the nitrogenous constituents of juice'.[34] The instability resulting from the accumulated nitrogen triggered 'similar instability into the sugar, hence fermentation'.[35]

This he saw as a product of decomposition rather than a transformation effected by the processes of a living organism.[36] Though Liebig's argument found some purchase, by the mid-nineteenth century most scientists came to agree with Cagniard de la Tour that yeast was alive and essential for a successful brew.

Pasteur would drive this point home in his 1860 treatise on alcohol fermentation. 'The chemical act of fermentation is essentially a phenomenon correlative with a vital act, commencing and ceasing with the latter,' he wrote. 'I am of the opinion that alcoholic fermentation never occurs without simultaneous organisation, development, multiplication of cells, or the continued life of cells already formed.'[37] For Pasteur, there was no fermentation without life, and in beer this life was yeast.

Though scientists aligned with Pasteur discussed yeast as if it were a singular entity, as a class of microorganism it was actually multitudinous. And although Pasteur recognized this fact, he never tried to isolate or taxonomize these organisms. 'I have never given specific names to these different yeasts,' he wrote in his memoir on diseases of beer, 'any more than to the other microscopic organisms that I have had occasion to study.'[38]

Pasteur did trouble himself, however, to identify those microbes which he thought to be responsible for beer spoilage. This task accomplished, he went on to attempt to develop what he considered a pure strain of yeast for brewing. He went, microscope in hand, to some London brewers who were dissatisfied with the quality of their porter. He showed them 'the presence of filaments peculiar to turned beer' and said the fault lay in the yeast culture.[39] To brew quality porter it was necessary to keep the culture pure. 'This method consists in proving that beer never possesses any unpleasant flavour,' he wrote,

> so long as the alcoholic ferment, properly so called, is not
> associated with foreign ferments; that this also holds good in

the case of wort, and that wort, liable to change as it is, may be preserved in a state of purity, if it is kept under conditions that protect it from the invasion of microscopic parasites, to which it presents not only favourable nutriment, but also a field for development.[40]

As it turned out, Pasteur's method of cultivating beer yeasts did not lend itself to a completely pure culture. With a sterile instrument he transferred a bit of culture to a sterile liquid medium. Fresh growth, so indicated by turbidity in the culture tube, he introduced to another sterile medium.[41] Done enough times, the process would result in a pure culture of one type of microorganism, Pasteur believed. What he glimpsed in his microscope appeared to confirm this. Yet the pure cultures almost always owed to dumb luck. Known today as 'enrichment cultures', they may add body, nose or flavour to beers, but their chance nature ill suits them to the creation of a brewing empire.[42]

Isolation of a world-conquering brewer's yeast would have to await the efforts of Emil Christian Hansen. Taking Pasteur's work on bacterial contamination a step further, Hansen arrived at two important findings. First, two kinds of yeast cooperated in brewing. Second, an intruding wild yeast may spoil a ferment. Hansen observed further that a strain of yeast was physiologically distinctive, even if it appeared quite like another strain. Like Hansen, Pasteur had noticed this. Unlike Hansen, however, he had not troubled to speculate as to the meaning of it. Hansen posited that two microorganisms otherwise identical in terms of size, shape and colour could cause different chemical reactions. With this in mind he set about developing methods for classifying and identifying the various yeast strains.

His task faced a real challenge: cross-contamination ran rampant. This much was brought home to him by the daily doings of the Carlsberg brewery workers. 'The spent yeast is spilled in the yard and carried down into fermentation cellars on the boots of the workers,' he noted, 'or it dries to dust out there, and is blown by the wind into the coolships.'[43] Thus the trouble began; for though the yeast initially develops slowly, so much wild yeast accumulated in the pitching yeast – the wort to which the yeast culture has been added – that it came to contaminate the entire batch. 'From that moment,' Hansen wrote, 'the development runs with tearing speed, and soon all the beer in the brewery will be infected.'[44]

In his brewery laboratory Hansen resisted the urge to work with tearing speed on a method of obtaining a pure culture. Under sterile conditions and over a moist chamber he placed a drop of yeast suspension on the underside of a cover glass bearing haemo-cytometer-like markings. If the drop contained, say, twenty cells, he added a drop of suspension of the same size to 40 ml (1.4 fl. oz) of water. He then introduced this greatly diluted suspension in 1 ml aliquots to flasks of sterile wort (unfermented beer). He left these flasks undisturbed to allow the few cells – perhaps no more than three – to sink to separate positions at the flask's bottom. After several days individual growths became evident. If Hansen observed that only one cell produced a growth, he concluded that he had isolated a pure culture.[45]

Hansen worked with a liquid medium, which was often difficult to control. As luck would have it, the renowned German bacteriologist Robert Koch had found an easier method. He wanted to study bacteria that grew readily in a medium of nutrient broth. The problem was that the medium was difficult to work with. But Koch hit upon a solution. He developed a way of converting the nutrient medium from a liquid to a solid. A real breakthrough, the method lent itself to all sorts of microorganisms and produced a pure culture so easily that almost anyone could reproduce it.[46] Moreover, it found other applications, such as assessing the number and kinds of microorganisms found in various samples – air, water, soil and, perhaps most importantly, food.[47]

Robert Koch at work in his laboratory, c. 1885. The esteemed German scientist's discovery of a method for the easy reproduction of various cultures led to breakthroughs in the field of bacteriology.

The secret to the method was silver salts. Koch substituted them for the nutrient medium used by Hansen and others. His sterile plates he kept under a bell jar in order to prevent contamination. These he inoculated with a needle or platinum wire, spreading the inoculum over the medium's entire surface. Koch let the bacteria incubate, and then he transferred them from the individual colonies to a nutrient gelatine in test tubes plugged with cotton. So novel was Koch's approach that even Pasteur, a patriotic Frenchman still stinging from his nation's loss to Germany, offered words of praise: 'C'est un grand progrès, Monsieur.'[48]

Koch published a paper on his methods in 1881, and it would become the 'Bible of Bacteriology'.[49] Koch criticized 'the Pasteur school' for its inaccurate methods, which, as he insisted, 'renders it doubtful that they have obtained in pure culture the organisms of rabies, sheep pox, tuberculosis, and so forth'.[50] 'The pure culture is the foundation for all research on infectious diseases,' he declared, and many took note.[51] In 1882 Hansen visited Koch's Berlin laboratory to improve his own method. Using the knowledge gained from this visit, Hansen cultivated cultures on set gelatine containing well-separated cells and kept under a cover glass. He used only colonies that developed from single cells to inoculate a sterile medium.[52]

Days were now numbered for the smelly, bitter beer plaguing the Carlsberg brewery. Because Hansen had already cultured several pure yeast strains from the brewery, he quickly fingered the culprit. He called it *Saccharomyces pastorianus*.[53] The brewery's yeast, arrived from Munich's Spaten Brewery some four decades prior, had become contaminated with an alien strain, one that matched a sample from a nearby orchard.[54] Earlier research having shown him that some yeast strains may produce unsavoury results, Hansen set about carrying out morphological and physiological studies on the pure cultures. The time required for sporulation at a certain temperature betrayed the presence of undesirable strains. He pointed out other typical traits, such as conditions of membrane formation and behaviour towards various carbohydrates, as well as differences in the results from fermentation.[55] On the basis of these traits he isolated four strains of *Saccharomyces* from the Carlsberg brewery yeast. Only one produced consistently tasty beer, and it became known as 'Carlsberg bottom yeast no. 1'. Finally, a pure culture had been achieved through a process that would allow breweries to standardize yeasts for reliable batches and avoid strains that produced off flavours.

J. C. Jacobsen reaped a generous return on his investment in Hansen's work. On 12 November 1883 the Old Carlsberg Brewery brewed its first batch of beer with the new, pure strain.[56] By 1884

Horse-drawn wagon delivering casks of Carlsberg beer to customers in and around Copenhagen, Denmark. Thanks to the breakthrough of the brewery's house microbiologist, Emil Hansen, the brewery's owner was able to ramp up production of a reliably high-quality beer for domestic and foreign markets.

the entire production run of 200,000 hectolitres (5.3 million u.s. gallons) contained Hansen's pure strains of yeast. The quality was such that the beer could satisfy demand domestically and abroad. And Jacobsen's confidence was such that he offered samples, free of charge, of the yeast responsible for his beer's quality. His might have been a poor business decision, because it revved up the brewing industry like nothing before. By 1888 Carlsberg bottom yeast no. 1 was in use in all the major breweries of Denmark and Norway, as well as breweries in Sweden, Finland, Austria-Hungary, Switzerland, Italy, France, Belgium and North America, not to mention Asia, Australia and South America.[57]

Hansen's career likewise revved up. The restless dreamer who began life caring for an alcoholic father and overworked mother now had scientists paying him court to learn the 'Hansen method'. Honorary doctorates from the universities of Uppsala, Geneva and the Vienna Technical College followed.[58] He was made a Knight of Dannebrog, a Danish order of chivalry, by King Christian IX and later a Commander of the Dannebrog by Christian's son and successor, King Frederick VIII. He received a gold medal from Carl Jacobsen, the son and successor of Carlsberg's founder. And when a brief illness sent him to his grave, he was honoured with a full-page obituary in *Nature* magazine.

\* \* \*

Technology became the brewing industry's primary asset. It had helped to domesticate *Saccharomyces cerevisiae* and deliver a level of quality previously unheard of for beer. But technology represented an enormous capital expense. Breweries that could not afford mechanical refrigeration, which came into use in the 1870s, or steam-driven machinery went under, leaving the market bereft of their unique offerings. The hundreds of beer varieties enjoyed by the Dutch, for instance, shrank to a few dozen. Brewing giants Whitbread and Barclay Perkins rose in London, and Guinness in Dublin. In the United States, St Louis-based Anheuser-Busch dominated the market.[59] Dark, hearty brews fell into disfavour as bright, bubbly lagers prevailed. The latter were tasty, yet somehow less interesting (only the Belgians remained true to the less predictable top-fermenting yeasts). Pasteurization, which brewers had adopted as a way of further controlling fermentation, and the use of cheap adjunct grains such as rice and corn dealt additional blows to the new beers' appeal. Standardization became the watchword. Production increased and variety decreased. Drab sameness and predictability crept into beer drinking.

And it became lonelier to boot. Bottling begun in the closing years of the nineteenth century afforded beer lovers the option of drinking at home. Gone was the excuse to run to the tavern for a pint and a few hours of after-work conviviality. By the mid-twentieth century, the television's glow was many beer drinkers' sole company.

Mid-20th-century poster advertisement for Rheingold Beer. The New York-based industrial brewery, which ceased operations in 1976, was one of many that leveraged earlier breakthroughs in reliable methods of producing lagers for a mass market.

As we will see, technology would become the primary asset of another industry. Bread, like beer, would go from home-made provision to commercial product once we had a better understanding of the microorganism essential to its making.

# 3 'Oven Worship':
## Bread and Its Various Preparations from Earliest Antiquity to the Present

'A loaf of bread', the Walrus said,
'is what we chiefly need.'
– Lewis Carroll, 'The Walrus and the Carpenter'[1]

THE METHODS DEVELOPED by Emil Hansen led to the description of 130 kinds of yeast between 1880 and 1900.[2] The knowledge gained revolutionized the production of wine, beer, bread and other foods. Yet the revolution would meet some resistance from those individuals who deemed yeast's presence in bread dangerous, and even deadly. And if they were not raising the alarm about this living leavening agent, they were pursuing ways of replacing it with a non-living substitute.

Eben Horsford counted himself one such yeast-phobe. In 1847 Horsford established the United States' first laboratory for analytical chemistry at Harvard University. There he devoted himself to the practical application of the sciences, taking his students on tours of local glassworks, soap factories, oil refineries and other sites of industrial production.[3] Yet through all this he felt himself something of an outsider, having neither attended as an undergraduate the school that employed him nor married a trustee or faculty member's daughter. His position he some-times found stifling; the opportunity to work elsewhere, therefore, understandably attracted him.

In 1854 Horsford went into business with George F. Wilson and J. B. Duggan, two men from Providence, Rhode Island. Among other things, they would make baking powders. At a site in Pleasant Valley, Rhode Island, in 1855 Wilson, Duggan & Co. – Horsford the 'Co.' – established a plant and swung into production.

Horsford's business-minded approach to science came from his mentor, the irrepressible Justus von Liebig, he who had wrangled so stubbornly with Pasteur. Horsford studied with Liebig from 1844 to 1846 and was only the second American at the time to have done so. The experience left a deep impression on him. His mentor taught him that chemistry's best use lies in improving the human condition and that the factory floor, rather than a university laboratory, best lent itself to doing so.

As it happened, Horsford had a head for business. In 1856, the year his Pleasant Valley plant opened, he received a patent for the manufacture of monocalcium phosphate, a chemical to replace cream of tartar in baking powder. This he combined with bicarbonate of soda (baking soda), christening the mixture 'yeast powder', though its properties had nothing in common with its namesake.

Horsford used the misnomer deliberately. Like Liebig, he thought yeast – indeed, all microscopic fungi – dangerous. In his work of 1861, *The Theory and Art of Bread-making*, he argues for the superiority of chemical leavening agents over natural ones. 'The ex-istence of microscopic organisms in the various forms of yeast has been established,' he writes: 'they are the incidental concomitants of decay.' Moreover, he continues, 'it is not difficult to conceive that the ferments and their yeast-plants, having escaped destruction by the heat of baking, may produce ill effects when they reach the general circulation.'[4] An outwardly innocuous loaf of bread could

Eben Horsford, the Harvard chemistry professor who believed that yeast was harmful, and thus its use in bread and similar foods was best avoided. To that end, he created the chemical alternative, baking powder, once he had left academia to join two business partners to found what would become known as the Rumford Chemical Works.

harbour millions of these offending putrescent bodies. There was simply no way of ensuring their complete absence short of avoiding their use altogether. Yeast had become enemy number one.

The growing uneasiness with biological leavening agents meant that Horsford's chemical alternative found a ready customer base. A revolution in hygiene had begun, and Wilson, Duggan & Co. meant to profit from it. So profitable had the outfit grown, in fact, that its principals felt moved to change its name. Rechristened Rumford Chemical Works in 1858, it continued the baking powder it made popular under its former moniker. The product graces supermarket shelves to this day.

Rumford's competitors likewise fastened on the idea of marketing through fear-mongering. Royal Baking Powder, another

The Rumford Chemical Works. Originally named Wilson, Duggan & Co., the company exploited the then-current belief that yeast was a harmful contaminant of bread in order to stoke demand for its artificial alternative, baking powder. It has enjoyed enduring success, as present-day supermarket shelves will readily attest.

major u.s. player in the industry, worked hard to convince the public that, in addition to keeping them from sickness, chemically leavened bread saved them time because it was easier to bake. Royal communicated this message in joke books, colouring books and song books, on paperweights and porcelain plates, and perhaps most effectively in proprietary cookbooks. The *Royal Baker and Pastry Cook*, for example, presents the company's take on yeast:

> Bread was first made without leaven, heavy and solid. Then yeast was discovered, and yeast-risen bread came into use throughout the civilized world. Finally baking powder was devised, the most healthful, economical, and convenient of all leavening or lightening agents.

A primitive precursor to baking powder, 'Yeast is a living plant,' the book continues. 'Mixed with dough it causes fermentation and destruction of a part of the flour' through the leavening process, whereas baking powder does 'precisely the same work' without

Cover of a proprietary cookbook by the Price Baking Powder Factory.
Publication of such cookbooks offered manufacturers opportunity to bring their
product to public consciousness while also normalizing its use in place of natural
yeast, which they routinely demonized.

the destruction. Moreover, 'there is no mixing or kneading with the hands, no setting of sponge overnight, as the loaf is mixed and ready for the oven at once.'[5] Domestic bakers stood to realize greater nutrition and convenience with baking powder.

The sally against yeast struck home in domestic bakers, who sought any excuse to move away from naturally leavened bread. Like most living things, yeast required certain conditions to flourish. Its leavening action moreover took time, and it needed a dough elastic enough to contain the carbon dioxide it produced, which meant much kneading to produce gluten. Baking powder, on the other hand, confronted bakers with no similar quirks. Chemical rather than biological, it acted predictably and reliably, leavening dough by releasing carbon dioxide gas through an acid–base reaction, usually between sodium bicarbonate and acid salts. This meant it could leaven weak, quickly mixed doughs with delightfully airy results and little effort. Developed with hygiene and convenience in mind, baking powder upended what had been the millennia-old state of breadmaking.

* * *

Convenient and predictable, baking powder threatened to eliminate the need for yeast from breadmaking. Nonetheless, for centuries the need for yeast was quite absolute, if risen bread was the goal. Admittedly, yeast could prove fiddly, as any living ingredient might. We ought, then, to consider this ingredient in its nature and behaviours and relate something of its eventual mastery by bakers.

In the simplest terms, yeast is an ovoid fungal cell that reproduces by forming buds.[6] It is unicellular and cannot move on its own, lacking flagella. And at a mere 0.004 mm in diameter – four times wider than a bacterium, and half the diameter of a red blood cell – it is small.

It also has something in common with us. Like human beings, yeast is eukaryotic, the nuclei of its cells containing DNA. But that's where the similarities end. When yeast feeds on sugar each microorganism swells for an hour or two and then squeezes a bud from its surface. Mother gives birth to daughter, and both bear a birth scar. Yet this is an anthropomorphism; yeast is neither male nor female. In reproduction, two versions of yeast, sexless and outwardly identical, form buds that emit distinctive chemical attractants. In short, a yeast cell finds the right reproductive partner by smell.[7]

Yeasts that make bread rise and beer alcoholic tend to upstage those which perform the humbler work of breaking down waste and recycling nutrients. Like bacteria, they are decomposers. And they are everywhere. An estimated 1 quadrillion yeast cells live in the world's rivers. More live in lakes, and many more yet in oceans. Indeed, yeasts make a home almost anywhere – fish viscera, deep-sea muds, sunken ships and even the walls of Chernobyl's ruined reactor. Leaves teem with them. One variety grows only in the stomachs of chinchillas. Other, less particular kinds grow in cheese, sausages, corpses and soil.[8] They grow in the frigid waters of melting glaciers and in the air. They like foggy weather, because the moisture lets them travel with greater ease. And some scientists speculate that yeast, together with fungal spores, stimulates the birth of raindrops.[9]

Yeasts also call us human beings home, living on our scalps and feet, in our nostrils and ear canals. This relationship begins at birth. We come into this world colonized by strains of the sometimes harmful yeast *Candida*: our mother's birth canal slathered us in it

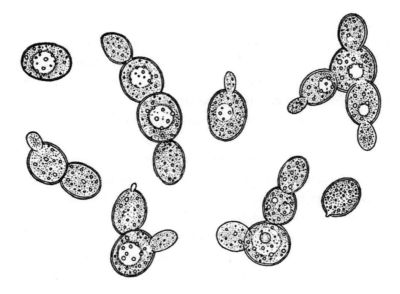

Reproducing yeast cells. The small prominences evident on several cells are daughter cells, also known as blebs or buds. These will mature into yeast cells that in turn engender more offspring.

Reproduction of yeast as sketched by Antonie van Leeuwenhoek, the 17th-century Dutch lens-maker who sparked a revolution in scientific understanding when his invention, the microscope, revealed a realm of vanishingly small organisms that had previously gone unseen.

as we passed. This is why babies sometimes develop a white over-growth of yeast in their mouths. As their microbiome adjusts, this flowering of yeast fades but does not disappear. Rather, *Candida* microbes are kept in check by the friendly bacteria that colonize our gut. When this balance is upset the result can be dangerous: an opportunistic yeast, the same strains of *Candida* cause everything from peritonitis, abdominal abscesses, endocarditis and meningitis to liver and blood infections and arthritis.[10]

Yeast will flourish just about anywhere that conditions permit, including human innards. In 2010 a 61-year-old Texas man entered an emergency room. Though he seemed intoxicated and was found to have an alarmingly high blood alcohol content of 0.37 per cent, he claimed to have had nothing to drink. And, indeed, he often appeared drunk without discernible cause. The episodes were more frequent whenever he missed a meal, exercised or had tippled the night before. His wife, a nurse, would regularly test his blood alcohol. It would sometimes be as high as 0.33 to 0.40 per cent, well above the United States' legal driving limit of 0.08 per cent. What had laid the hapless Texan low was *Saccharomyces cerevisiae*, the yeast for brewing beer and baking bread. High levels of it had infected him after a course of antibiotics years earlier had depleted him of the microbes that usually keep yeast in check. The invasive yeast fermented the sugars in the food he ingested into alcohol and carbon dioxide. In short, his digestive tract had become a brewery. A low-carbohydrate diet and a course of antifungal drugs eventually brought him relief.[11]

Yeast's eager fecundity did not escape notice. Some astute soul sensed that a bit of dough trimmed from a loaf going into the oven would cause any new dough added to it to also effervesce. That soul further noticed that once it had established itself in, say, bread dough, grape must or beer wort, it would continue to work its magic for generations if it regularly received fresh amounts of that medium. Breadmaking thereafter became as much a part of ordinary life as sleeping and eating.

The Egyptians were the first to direct fermentation to the larger purpose of feeding a growing population. They bred an easily husked variety of wheat (earlier wild strains required parching in order to husk grains, a process that denatured the gluten-forming proteins) whose flour held together when leavened.[12] Yet getting to this stage took hard work. Bread often meant great labour. Women, slaves and captives did the work of milling grain. The long drudgery left its mark. Skeletons unearthed from this period show squatting facets on leg bones from hours spent bent to the task. The later invention and use of rotary querns – simple mills consisting of two stones – eased the task a bit. But it was still taxing work. Kneading likewise required great physical effort. A relief in the tomb of Ramses III, who died in 1156 BCE, shows two men kneading dough with their feet as they keep themselves upright with long sticks.[13]

The variety of breads that were available in Egypt is impressive. During the time of the New Kingdom (c. 1539–1075 BCE) an Egyptian could choose from more than forty different breads. The rich ate white bread, which they would flavour with sesame seeds,

Rendering of reliefs depicting ancient Egyptian breadmakers in attitudes characteristic of their trade. Despite the difficult work, which left lasting physical effects, they managed to bring to market a considerable variety of offerings.

butter and fruit. The poor ate brown bread, often of barley, which they took plain. Along with wheat and barley, emmer, spelt and a sort of millet known as dourah were used in bread.[14] Some breads were paper-thin; others, thick and hearty.

Constant refinements and additions to making and baking point to the utter centrality of bread to ancient Egyptian society. No mere staple, bread made manifest a sovereign's power; he (or she) apportioned it to those who lacked the means of making it. Slave, peasant, priest and warrior alike ate it. It was given in payment to the workers who built the pyramid of Cheops (c. 2575–2465 BCE). For the twelve to eighteen hours they worked hauling massive blocks of limestone they received a wage of three loaves, two measures of beer and some onions and radishes. Valour could win additional loaves for the individual who displayed it. The legendary hero Dedi received five hundred loaves of bread daily to go with the one hundred jars of beer he was also given. And prevailing mores ensured that even beggars would not go without. 'Do not eat bread when another is standing near without holding out your hand to offer some to him,' went an Egyptian adage. Wise pharaohs hoarded bread in anticipation of lean times ahead – a hedge as much against any loss of their power as any loss of subjects to starvation. Genesis 47:13–27 relates how, after famine had struck, word of a providential stockpile of grain in Egypt reached neighbouring peoples, who begged the pharaoh to share it with them.[15]

The Egyptians understood the importance of bread; the Romans came to understand the importance of the baker. Pliny the Elder records that professional bakers established themselves in Rome in the second century BCE. Greeks, slaves, freedmen and individuals otherwise on the margins of Roman society formed a craft guild, which offered companionship in the form of communal dinners and, more importantly, aid against financial ruin. And, indeed, guild members often prospered. One of the largest and best-preserved examples of a freedman's funerary monument, the tomb of baker Marcus Vergilius Eurysaces (50–20 BCE) features lavish bas-reliefs depicting details of his profession. In one, a donkey drives a paddle standing upright in a clay vessel. In another, a baker with a peel removes loaves from an ovular oven. In yet

Detail of a relief adorning the tomb of the Roman baker Eurysaces. The trade enabled individuals on the margins of Roman society to achieve comfortable respectability and enjoy the benefits of solidarity and mutual aid, these last owing to a thriving bakers' guild.

another, loaves are stacked and weighed. That Eurysaces could erect such a memorial to himself and his profession offers a sense of the importance of bread to Roman society.[16]

Bread was as abundant as it was important. Few went without it. The poor got theirs free, whereas the rich had to pay. (The exotic added ingredients made the price worth it.) Not even war interrupted the supply; soldiers took with them portable bread-making equipment. Lest misfortune strike, bringing with it a poor harvest or some other event that might make bread scarce, Romans turned to petitioning or propitiating their deities. They worshipped Fornax, patroness of ovens and one of their most important mother goddesses.[17] And each year they held a festival for the grain goddess Ceres, who presided over the harvest and the circle of life and death. A celebration of great splendour and beauty, it included slaves, women and children. Everyone took part in it, for everyone ate bread.

Romans did not stand alone historically in their reverence for bread. Greeks of classical antiquity celebrated the spring festival of Thargelia, in which the gods Artemis and Apollo received bread as an offering. Christians regarded bread as the body of Christ transubstantiated; to defile it was considered a great sacrilege. And Jews, though they did not engage in 'oven worship', recognized the divine favour that produced bread, speaking as they broke it the *berakhah* (blessing), 'Blessed art Thou, O Lord our God, who bringest forth bread out of the ground.'

God may have brought bread from the ground, but it required mills to get it to the table. Mills replaced the women and slaves who ground grain by hand. Their size and essential role in the process often made them objects of wonder, and even great mistrust. Barbarians saw the Roman miller as an evil magician who tortured the water that washed over his wheel. Confirmation of this perception came in the form of occasional mill explosions, which happened whenever clouds of flour sufficiently dense –

Woodcut of a medieval miller plying his trade. An object of mistrust owing to his suspected dishonesty, he nonetheless performed an indispensable service to his community.

20 g or more suspended in every square metre of air – combusted on meeting the frictional heat generated by turning millstones.[18]

Yet few dared to damage a mill; its flour sustained the community as the very staff of life. In Bruegel's 1564 painting *The Procession to Calvary*, a mill sits atop a craggy mountain, commanding a position from which its occupant, the miller, may survey all. Though central to town life, a mill often stood well outside town walls. For this reason the social position of the miller was that of an outsider, albeit an indispensable one. He made flour largely out of the view of his fellow townspeople, and thus they never quite knew what went on within his mill. They suspected him of stealing grain entrusted to him or overcharging them for milling it. The fourteenth-century English poet Geoffrey Chaucer made such misdeeds famous in *The Canterbury Tales*, in which he writes of one of his pilgrims, the miller: 'Wel koude he stelen corn and tollen thries; / And yet he hadde a thombe of gold, pardee.' His thumb was 'gold' because he used it to pad his fee by pressing it on the scale as he weighed a customer's grain.

Only slightly higher in his fellow townsfolk's regard stood a baker. Roman bakers' guilds waned as the Empire did before disappearing altogether with the barbarian invasions and subsequent onset of the Dark Ages. Yet the Middle Ages saw them rise again. The Great Pipe Roll of Henry II records the organization of City of London bakers into a guild. This they did in 1155, dividing the guild into two groups, bakers of brown bread in one and bakers of white in the other.[19] Both occupied an important position in cities and towns. A thirteenth-century Germanic book of common law, the *Sachsenspiegel*, put the fine for a baker's murder at three times the fine for an ordinary man's.[20] Though invaluable to a town, a baker was not beloved by it. 'When the poor man weeps, the baker laughs,' went a Spanish proverb. Like millers, bakers laboured under a cloud of suspicion. They were thought to cheat customers by selling loaves that weighed too little or were made with inferior flour.

Sovereigns throughout Europe brought needed oversight to renascent baking guilds of the Middle Ages. Henry III's Assize of Bread and Ale of 1266 regulated the price, weight and quality of bread and beer manufactured and sold in towns, villages and hamlets. The first British food law of its kind, it required a baker to stamp his loaves with a unique mark for the purpose of tracing any inferior ones to him. These he could have hung around his neck as he was dragged through the streets in punishment. An offending baker also faced fines or even the loss of his baking privileges altogether. Penalties varied by region. In 1280 angry citizens of

Zurich placed a baker in a large basket, which they then hung over a puddle. Known as a baker's gallows, it offered its prisoner only one way of escape: a leap into the muddy water below him. For the indignity the baker exacted revenge by setting half the town afire. 'Tell the people of Zurich,' he reportedly shouted as he carried out his terrible deed, 'I wanted to dry my clothes, which were still wet from the puddle.'[21]

If the occupation of baker bred mistrust, it also bred unremitting toil. Little changed since its inception in ancient Egypt. An apprenticeship lasted three to four years and was followed by a journeyman period of another five years or so in which a baker wandered from town to town ostensibly to learn new techniques, though really to keep from competing with his master. After such time any vacancy he hoped to fill – be it that of a baker of white, brown, sweet or sourdough bread – required that he fete guildsmen bakers with a banquet and swear to uphold the town's existing bread ordinances. He pledged that he would always bake enough to keep the villagers supplied and mind regulations governing the quality and weight of his product. For his trouble he won to himself a lifetime of working up to eighteen hours a day (bakers were the only tradesmen allowed to work through the night) and breathing flour dust. Dust aspirated over a long period could bring on asthma, bronchial catarrh, stiffening and shortening of the knees (the so-called 'baker's knee') and a kind of eczema that attacked the sebaceous glands of the biceps and chest.[22]

As the centuries passed, perception of bakers changed. Grain became more plentiful as crops became more predictable, lessening somewhat the temptation to cheat. Sentimentality thus overtook suspicion as it concerned the baking trade. 'There was no place quite so welcome on a cold day as the bakehouse,' recalled twentieth-century British writer H. S. Joyce of his father's Dorset village bakery. 'If it was really cold weather, many of those who would claim any sort of acquaintance with Father, turned off the road and went into the bakehouse to enjoy the warmth, and have a chat before continuing their journey.'[23] Yet one thing remained – the long, hard work that was baking. And much of this work involved controlling the often inscrutable and volatile conditions necessary for making excellent bread.

\* \* \*

The bakers of Europe, hard-pressed though they were, developed hundreds of varieties of bread. Each village and town had its signature offerings. Many were made with a bit of leavened dough set aside from an earlier bake. Such bread – sourdoughs, essentially – had an enchanting aroma and taste, complex and full-bodied. Other breads were made with yeast from breweries and developed subtle flavours from dough that slowly rose overnight. Once ready, the dough would be shaped into all sorts of forms. The bakers

Australian men eating dampers with their tea. A rugged bread that consisted of flour, water, baking soda and sometimes milk, it represented the perfect ration for long forays in remote wilderness.

of Basel in Switzerland made a large star-shaped bread called *Bierschildlein* ('beer sign'), and those of Madrid in Spain made a small round bread that they pierced with a needle, the hole probably a vent for steam.

Other areas of the world also developed toothsome breads, the form and preparation of which were perfectly suited to the locale. Dough for Australian 'dampers', a soda bread, was mixed on sheets of bark. Rough and ready, a damper resembled its baker, a man making camp in the bush. Of him Emil Braun writes in *The Baker's Book* of 1903, 'kneeling amid the emphatic silence of nature, disturbed if at night only by the hideous howl of the dingo, or by day, the screech of the parrot of cockatoo, or the measured hopping of the kangaroo, he mixes [his] ingredients.' The bread he bakes over a fire made of eucalyptus, on a 'damper bed' which he has cleared. Ten minutes or so later, the bread is done, and the bush baker eats it with corned beef or fresh mutton purchased at the last station he visited.[24]

The warm, humid climate of southern India, meanwhile, does not suit the baking of large loaves in the European style. There such dough rises – and subsequently collapses – too quickly to be practical. Dominant in the region instead are smaller, rice-based breads. Spongy *idli*, for example, is made from a batter of rice and dehulled black gram – the seed of a native legume – which is steamed and shaped in round moulds. The batter's mucilaginous quality, imparted to it by the black gram, in turn imparts to the baked result a springy, honeycombed texture. Idli's thin and crispy counterpart, *dosa*, is made from a batter likewise consisting of black gram and rice that ferments ten to sixteen hours before it is baked in a sizzling greased pan.[25]

Bakers of idli and dosa made the best of their tropical situation. The fermented batters of these breads teem with lactic acid bacteria as well as three or four kinds of yeast, all of which are introduced by the two constituent ingredients, rice and black gram. African bakers occupying similar latitudes boast breads equally as populous. *Koko* and *kenkey*, two Ghanaian breads, are made according to a similar process. Sorghum, millet or maize is steeped in water for one or two days, then it is ground into dough and fermented. The dough lends itself to a couple of preparations: it might be served as a thick porridge or as baked balls. The latter are made by moulding the dough, wrapping it in banana leaves and boiling it.[26] Much the same process informs the preparation of *injera*, an Ethiopian bread. From *teff*, a grain native to the country, is made batter, which is backslopped with *ersho*, a yellowish liquid formed on the batter of an earlier bake. The inoculated batter ferments for two or three days before it is baked on a large griddle.

Whereas Indian and African home bakers depended largely on backslopping and spontaneous fermentation for leavening their bread batters, their counterparts in England and Europe often relied on yeast from commercial breweries and bakeries, of which there were many. In pre- and post-revolutionary North America, meanwhile, bakers experimented with more unusual ways of leavening bread. Yeast could be had only by going to some trouble; commercial breweries and bakeries were scarce, and sourdough leavens enjoyed little appeal beyond pioneers and other sorts accustomed to roughing it. For these reasons no single standard applied when it came to leavening. Rather, cookbooks gave various methods of doing so. 'Two wine-glasses of the best brewer's yeast, or three of good home-made yeast,' recommends one tome from the era. A prescribed method might cause bread to come out tasting bitter or sour, or with some other defect. And a failed leaven represented a minor disaster, because bread was a dietary mainstay. A family of four consumed, on average, some 12.7 kg (28 lb) of the stuff a week, or slightly less than half a kilogram (1 lb) per person per day.[27]

High demand for bread and limited supplies of yeast inspired American housewives to experiment with chemical leavening agents well before the advent of easy-to-use baking powders. Such forerunners, however, did not much surpass yeast. In 1790 Samuel Hopkins of Vermont applied for a patent for 'an improved method of making pure pearl ash from wood ashes'.[28] This was potassium carbonate, an early lye-based leaven made from fire ashes boiled in cast-iron kettles down to 'salts' and scorched to remove any remaining vegetal matter. The remaining product had a grainy texture and yellow-grey hue. A more refined version arrived to market after Hopkins had applied for his patent, wholesale clearing of primeval forests for farmland amply supplying the raw material.

Because it imparted a delightful airiness and crispness, pearl ash found its way into baked goods other than bread. It is the leavening agent in the first published recipe in which the word 'cookies' appears. And it found use abroad. In 1792 alone the United States exported some 8,000 tons of pearl ash to Europe.[29]

Pearl ash took its place alongside other chemical leavening agents – acids, alkalis, mineral salts and various mixtures and admixtures of these things. Similarly popular was spirit of harts-horn (and it remains so in Scandinavian countries, where it is used to make thin, crisp cookies). Approximately 28.5 per cent ammonia distilled from deer antlers, it was sold in lumps for grinding into powder.

Further refinement in the art of making chemical leavening agents would fall to big business. Church & Dwight, the company that would later become Arm & Hammer, brought baking soda (bicarbonate of soda) to market in 1846. Known formally as sodium bicarbonate, the new product soon surpassed other leavening agents, which could cause unpleasant flavours. In popularity it matched potassium bicarbonate, or saleratus, as consumers knew it. This name potassium bicarbonate shared with pearl ash (nomenclature of the time muddied distinctions on occasion). Ten years later Eben Horsford would hit upon the idea of combining sodium bicarbonate with monocalcium phosphate, creating the chemical yeast substitute familiar to us living today, baking powder.

Housewives embraced Horsford's innovation; the agent saved them the time they would otherwise have had to devote to proving bread and cake dough with yeast. Leavening with yeast, a living microorganism, was a biological matter and therefore entailed ministrations and care. Leavening with baking soda, saleratus and the like, on the other hand, was a matter of basic chemistry. From a few ingredients could be made quite a number of goods. Pancakes, cookies, waffles, biscuits, cupcakes, fritters – all these and more were now possible with chemical leavening agents. No longer must days be spent in making large, heavy bread loaves that dominated the table for weeks (large loaves kept better than small). These smaller, lighter foods could be prepared and eaten when the whim struck. They were akin to the new flood of consumer items and experiences coming on to the market, as easily had as, say, a new pair of gloves or a visit to the carnival. In middle-class homes they occasioned such new events as afternoon tea parties and other festive gatherings, providing a welcome entertainment outlet to otherwise overburdened homemakers.[30]

Chemical leavening agents helped to bring about a shift in the way people thought about cooking and eating. The preparation of food had previously been largely a partnership between the cook and certain natural laws and microorganisms, one that entailed understanding earned through long observation. Little emphasis fell on economizing in the act of cooking or on subordinating it to other activities.

As the eighteenth century ended and the nineteenth began, however, time came to take on a different meaning. The American anthropologist and social critic David Graeber writes that with the Industrial Revolution arrived an inducement 'to see time as did the medieval merchant: as a finite property to be carefully budgeted and disposed of, much like money'. 'What's more,' he continues, 'the new technologies [of the period] also allowed any person's fixed time on earth to be chopped up into uniform units that could be bought and sold *for* money.'[31]

Uncertain, temperamental and often slow-acting, yeast as a leavening agent meant an inordinate amount of time lost to baking. Chemical agents, on the other hand, accelerated and standardized leavening, thus enabling bakers to allot an exact amount of time to the task. As the mindset of Graeber's medieval merchant took hold generally, the poor came to see their plight in a new light. Time was money, and those with little of either feared that any unremunerative activity could only add to their difficulties.

Print advertisement for baking powder. Affordable, quick and reliable, baking powder became the leavening agent of choice (or, indeed, necessity) for the impoverished and downtrodden, who were experiencing the time-crunch visited on them by industrialism. Waged work in factories meant many hours away from home and its attendant duties, baking among them. Baking powder thus offered expediency and convenience. Yet these virtues came at the expense of the superior flavour and nutrition of breads baked according to tradition.

The middle classes could fill the time they saved by using chemical leaveners as they wished; the poor and subjugated had it filled for them. When in 1877 the U.S. government dispossessed the native Zuni people of their ancestral land, placing them on a reservation, it replaced their corn and other staple foods with white flour, sugar, baking powder and oil. With these ingredients the Zuni made the fry bread so familiar at southwestern roadsides today, which is not nearly as nutritious as their traditional blue-corn bread, the recipe for which was passed from mother to daughter according to custom.[32] In this fate they joined their dispossessed fellows across the Atlantic, the Irish. Impoverished by onerous rents, the Irish subsisted on the soda bread that replaced buttery oatcakes and other more nourishing foods. Only the monied could now afford to savour the ancestral loaf.

*　*　*

For the dispossessed and rent-squeezed, chemically leavened bread was simply a fact of life. As concerned as they may have felt, they could do little about its lack of nutrients or its consequent impact on their health. Curiously, however, their wealthier counterparts in America and Europe joined them in fretting about its health effects. The nineteenth-century Presbyterian minister Sylvester Graham spoke of the moral purity of wholewheat bread and a vegetarian diet. Yet he deemed traditional breads no more beneficial. He called yeast an 'impure and poisonous substance'.[33] If it must be used it ought to be fresh and sourced locally.

Another health advocate, Dr William Alcott, went even further than Graham, cautioning his readers to avoid fermented bread altogether. Fermentation was putrefaction, he insisted, and yeast a decayed substance harmful to the human body. Yet he may have pursued his case beyond the bounds of palatability, even edibility. As an alternative to fermented bread and its evils, he touted an unsalted, unbolted and unleavened bread that he himself found difficult to swallow, writing of it: 'It appeared to me not merely tasteless and insipid, like bran and sawdust, but positively disgusting.'[34] The old notion of fermentation as putrefaction nonetheless prevailed, the many findings that suggested otherwise notwithstanding. The people behind the Boston Water Cure hazarded their own alternative in 1858, the year they published their pamphlet 'Good Bread: How to Make It Light, Without Yeast, or Powders'. Bread of their own time they decried therein as 'rotted by fermentation or poisoned with acids and alkalis' so thoroughly that 'the staff of life has well nigh become the staff of death'.[35] They suggested that bakers use an extremely hot oven in lieu of leavened dough; water expansion caused by the high temperature would in turn cause baking loaves to puff up.

As with the invention of chemical leavening agents as a replacement for yeast, the invention of ways of avoiding leavening altogether awaited stirrings of the entrepreneurial spirit. One individual moved by this spirit was John Dauglish. A London physician and member of the Chemical Society, he sought to harness vapours, steam and gases – sources of power much in vogue in Victorian Britain – as a means of performing the same work on bread dough as was done by yeast or chemical agents. He settled on carbon dioxide, which he captured by pouring sulphuric acid over calcium carbonate, that is, chalk. (He would later replace the acid and chalk with a 'wine whey' of fermented malt and flour.) The carbon dioxide released in the interaction aerated a fluid to be mixed with flour for the bread dough. Dauglish put the dough inside a giant, imposing iron ball containing, as the Victorian homemaker extraordinaire Mrs Beeton wrote, 'a system of paddles, perpetually turning, and doing the kneading part of the business' on activation of the ball's mechanisms.[36]

Thus was born the Aerated Bread Company, which its founder claimed had the capacity for converting in 40 minutes two sacks of flour, each weighing 560 lb (254 kg), into four hundred loaves

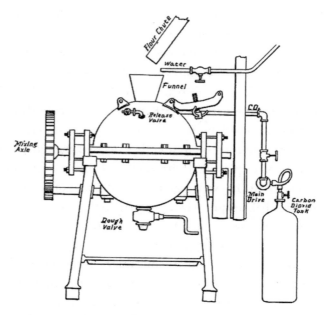

Schematic diagram of Dauglish's aerated bread machine. An early example of industry adapted to baking, loaves of aerated bread could be made quickly and in large number, and much of their nutritional value survived the process. Aerated bread nonetheless failed to catch on with consumers, because absent from it were the flavours that fermentation imparted to traditional doughs.

weighing 2 lb (0.9 kg) each. No doubt, many found the speed, economy and volume of Dauglish's invention duly impressive. At the very least it marked a huge improvement in terms of time saved over the ten hours or so needed for baking bread the traditional way. Along with time, nutrition was saved; bread made according to Dauglish's process reportedly remained high in carbohydrates. Yet those same carbohydrates went to nourishing yeast in traditionally leavened bread, and well-nourished yeast gave bread flavour. Aerated bread, on the other hand, was as insipid as it was costly to produce. It was a commercial flop, an outcome perhaps made even more inevitable by the fact that aerating equipment often behaved unpredictably and injured its operators.

Yet innovation did not cease with the failure of Dauglish's steamed bread. It rushed ever onward, the lure of money providing the impetus. And some of its fruits were happy. As an answer to chemical and mechanical methods of breadmaking, a domesticated form of yeast made its appearance in 1876 at Philadelphia's Centennial Exposition. It was the brainchild of two brothers from Vienna, Austria, who bore the surname Fleischmann and were disappointed in the quality of yeast available in the United States. Prior to their discovery, yeast had been a volatile ingredient. It was commonly kept in bottles, which often resulted in explosion, or it was dried and layered on a board, on which it sat exposed only to become contaminated. The inspired notion that perhaps compressing yeast would preserve it took hold of the Fleischmann brothers, and they acted on it, removing liquid from the stuff for pressing into small solid cakes. They found that yeast processed in this way stored and travelled well. Moreover, it lent itself to reliable bakes, left no bitter aftertaste and halved proving times. The Fleischmann brothers' gift to bakers commercial and domestic was a great boon.

Trade card from the turn of the 20th century advertising Fleischmann's yeast. Rendered shelf-stable and easily transported by the Fleischmann brothers' process, yeast finally came to join baking powder in the distinction of being a reliable time- and money-saving leavener.

For the first time in history they had at their disposal yeast that matched baking powder in terms of dependability and durability.[37]

Shelf-stable yeast joined a host of other innovations that responded to their moment. Yet many found they had little time for baking even bread leavened with baking powders or the Fleischmann brothers' fast-acting processed yeast. There consequently sprang up market demand for bread baked and ready to serve, and industry intervened to meet it. As loaves came to be made industrially, old ways of baking began to disappear – and with them their customary constraints. Though there lived on an expectation that a 'standard loaf' weigh either 2 or 4 lb (0.9 or 1.8 kg), the final repeal of the Assize of Bread in 1866 left bakers free to charge what they would. At the same time, the final dissolution of bakers' guilds sent wages plummeting, their rules and regulations no longer in force, and compelled bakers to compete solely on the bases of quality and price. The trade became crowded and unremunerative; barriers to entry, which the guilds had erected and enforced, fell, permitting just about anyone to set up shop.[38]

In response to the unwonted market pressures and regulatory easing, bakers turned to machines as a way of saving on labour costs. Resort to a technological solution served to transform baking into a capital-intensive endeavour. Whereas in years past bakers might get their dough mixed by employing family members, by around 1910 they had come to prefer kneading machines to cousins and in-laws. This preference was not shared by their traditionally minded contemporaries, however, who insisted that if kneading machines did not destroy dough outright, they seriously marred it.[39]

Indeed, it may be said that machine-mixed dough did contain a larger amount of water than dough mixed by hand. Also marred were the prospects of any aspiring bakers of modest means. Producers that could afford the high upfront costs of industrial baking equipment came to dominate the market. And where they could not quell complaints of poor quality, they answered with robust advertising campaigns aimed at establishing their product as a type of bread in its own right, distinct from any local, traditional bread that it may recall.[40] 'Don't just say "brown" – say Hovis', read one advertising slogan for a commercial wholemeal bread baker still popular in the UK today.

Commercial breadmaking on an industrial scale took a massive leap forward in 1961 with the British Baking Industries Research Association's Chorleywood process, which took loaves of bread from flour to packaging in three and a half hours. In its celerity the Chorleywood process improved on bulk fermentation, at five hours theretofore the speediest way of proving dough. Gluten development through resting dough gave way to development hustled through, as Elizabeth David noted, 'a few minutes of intense mechanical agitation in high-speed mixers'.[41] Loaves from dough submitted to the Chorleywood process came out firm yet spongy. And they travelled well because they sprang back to their original shape whenever they were squeezed. Yet they were insipid, because the yeast in them did not have time to produce the esters and other by-products that impart flavour.

The industrial triumph that was the Chorleywood process has endured into the present. Some 80 per cent of bread sold in Britain today is made by way of it. Commercial breadmakers in the United States, meanwhile, prefer the sponge-dough method, which despite a longer proving time is just as mechanical. Whatever the process, uniformly spongy, springy, insipid bread conquered the market, dooming wholesome, flavourful, artisanal bread to boutique appeal.

How did this come to pass? 'After 1900 we enter the period when anonymous corporations penetrate nearly every province of living,' writes the twentieth-century Swiss historian and critic Siegfried Giedion in his brilliant work of 1948, *Mechanization Takes Command*. 'Uniformity and the increasing stress on appearance entered hand in hand.'[42] Swept in the train of this corporate penetration was the staff of life itself. 'The changed characteristics of

Mid-20th-century print advertisement for the Bond brand of 'homogenized' bread. As the Chorleywood process and other innovations shortened and standardized breadmaking, corner bakeries lost ground to commercial giants, which had capital and resources enough to afford the specialized equipment necessary to meet the demand for ready-made bread among increasingly urban, wage-earning consumers.

bread always turned out to the benefit of the producer,' Giedion continues. 'It was as if the consumer unconsciously adapted his taste to the type of bread best suited to mass production and rapid turn-over.'[43]

Like any adaptation, that of consumers' taste in bread likely responded to environmental pressures. Drawn to large cities in search of opportunity, compelled to work twelve to sixteen hours a day and sleep during what hours remained, eaters of factory-made bread were themselves slaves to the factory. 'Bread and marg' became the working-class mainstay, a diet hardly conducive to good health. (And the bread had to be white and not wheat, for factory owners did not want their hands taking bathroom breaks.) As culinary historian Linda Civitello has observed, mass-produced baked goods had no history.[44] This very quality appealed to individuals whose need to seek work outside the home had alienated them from their own personal and familial histories. The bread available to them came to resemble the very nature of their labour in an industrial-age wage system – monotonous, without savour or distinction, cheaply acquired. The homey, hearth-baked loaf of their forebears, meanwhile, went from humble to exalted by dint of those very qualities. In light of an emergent culture of 'conspicuous consumption', so named by twentieth-century American sociologist Thorstein Veblen, the staples of pre-industrial commoners, prepared by hand with care if for no other reason than a lack of an alternative, had become 'artisanal' creations for purchase by members of the newly monied classes.

Artisanal bread vendor's stand at a farmer's market near Washington, DC.
Recent years have seen a vogue for traditional methods of baking. Artisanal breads appeal to consumers who appreciate the subtle yet distinct flavours of breads of yesteryear, and who also appreciate their nutritional benefits.

Advocates of processed food point to gains in convenience and quantity as support for their position. Yet the value of time recovered from work and other drudgery lies in the disposition of that time. If the beneficiaries may use it in indulging their passions, developing their talents, or securing their interests, then, yes, a gain has been made. If, however, they must devote it merely to more work, then the gains are anything but.

It bears asking also what has been lost in making these ostensible gains. Recent studies have shown that sourdough cultures and other natural leavens produce bread that ranks lower than bread produced by industrial methods on the glycaemic index – it is less likely to spike its eater's blood sugar – and higher in terms of the amount of bioavailable nutrients contained in it.[45] Traditionally fermented bread may even reduce gluten intolerance.[46] The subtle but vital magic of the microorganisms, whose pace of work is uncertain and in tune with the larger world of seasons and temperature, brings food from unwholesomeness to wholesomeness – an unqualified gain that trumps many others.

# 4 A Sometimes Dicey Duality: *Fungi and Food*

Molds were on the scene and doing well long before man appeared, and many of them are pretty certain to be around in the remote future, long after man has played his part and groped his way into the dark wings or fallen through the trapdoor on the stage.
– Clyde M. Christensen, *The Molds and Man: An Introduction to the Fungi*[1]

THE DISCOVERY THAT YEAST could leaven dough was felicitous. And not long thereafter it was found mould too could produce delights of its own. The story goes that a shepherd in southern France liked to nap in a certain cave. One day he woke and exited in pursuit of an attractive young shepherdess who had happened by, forgetting to take with him leftovers from his lunch of a cheese sandwich. There these leftovers sat until he returned sometime later. The sandwich's bread had become mouldy, and the shepherd cast it aside. He did venture, however, to sample the leftover cheese within. Its flavour he found greatly improved. On returning to his village he alerted his friends and neighbours to his discovery. Intrigued by his report, they brought their own cheese sandwiches to this same cave, left them and waited for the magic to happen.

Happen it did. Rich in a bacterial strain that has since come to be known as *Penicillium roqueforti*, the cave's soil contaminated the bread, which in turn dosed the cheese sandwiched in it. The latter grew blue mould. That cheese was, naturally, Roquefort. (It continues to be made in the shepherd's cave and others like it.)

Whether Roquefort was truly discovered in this picturesque way has not been established definitively. But the cheese likely was the result of fortuitous contamination. 'The first production of this cheese was just a happy accident,' wrote the twentieth-century American mycologist Clyde M. Christensen. 'The cheese makers were just trying to make the same cheese their forefathers had made, full of filth and flavour and nourishment.'[2]

Today some six hundred strains of *P. roqueforti* provide flavour and nourishment in a vast variety of cheeses. Though many cheese manufacturers rely on laboratory strains, some cling to tradition, leaving large loaves of overbaked rye bread in caves to be inoculated with mould, which they then powder and sprinkle on cheese curd or inject into holes made in the rind. (Roquefort and other interior mould cheeses are left unpressed, and the fissures and cracks thus remaining in the curd offer space and air for mould to grow.) The cheese is then left in caves until the mould thoroughly colonizes it. What emerges from the caves are the wonderful fragrant cheeses, such as Camembert, Gorgonzola and Stilton, beloved to this day.[3]

Cheese, which receives more in-depth discussion in Chapter Six, represents just one of many fermented foods which mould plays a feature role in making. A common grey mould called *Botrytis cinerea* helps to produce some of the world's most esteemed wines, for example. It often infects vineyards, causing the grapes to shrivel. Long considered a blight, it was discovered by an absent-minded German abbot in the late eighteenth century to

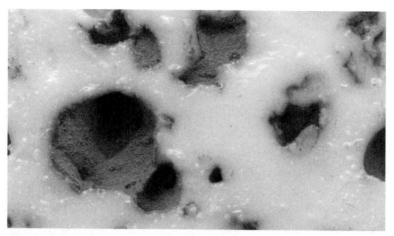

Close-up of a section of Roquefort cheese. In the recesses appear the cheese's characteristic mould, *P. roqueforti*. Though the cheese's origin story is probably apocryphal, the source of the cheese's mould is quite real. In fact, Roquefort continues to be made in the very cave in which the amorous shepherd is said to have napped.

be anything but. The vineyards in Germany then were owned by the Church, which decreed that no one could harvest grapes until the prince-abbot gave official word to begin. One year he appeared to have forgotten the harvest. The monks of the Bavarian town of Johannisberg awaited the appearance of the prince-abbot's messenger. Weeks passed and the grapes ripened. Wracked with worry, the monks sent a messenger of their own to the prince-abbot. But, as the story goes, this man was detained by either a highwayman or a comely woman, depending on the version, and never returned. The monks sent a second messenger who likewise vanished. A third was dispatched, made it to the prince-abbot, and returned with word of the latter's consent. The consent secured, the harvest could begin, albeit four weeks late. By then the above-mentioned mould had struck the overripe grapes. Nonetheless, the monks had a quota to make and both plump and shrivelled grapes were tossed in the wagons.

Grapes infected with *Botrytis cinerea*. Known colloquially as 'noble rot', it had long been considered a blight. Yet, thanks to the duress some medieval monks came under to fill a quota of wine, it was discovered that the fungus actually made for uniquely palate-pleasing varietals.

Happily, the seemingly destructive mould concentrated the sugars in the grapes and imparted unique notes of its own. It thus became known as the 'noble rot'. Europe's best vineyards today leave some grapes unpicked until *Botrytis* has done its work. They have even cultivated special strains of wine yeasts to complement the mould's terroir. Picolit, Gewürztraminer, Vouvray and Château d'Yquem – the last widely considered the finest of the lot – are made with botrytized grapes.[4]

The case of *Botrytis cinerea* offers an apt portrait of mould's sphinx-like nature. Is it friend or foe? The answer in the time before modern science could come only by way of experimentation and long experience. When it settles on rice, barley and soybeans, the filamentous mould of the genus *Aspergillus*, for example, reveals itself as friendly. The inoculated medium is known as *koji*, which means 'mouldy grains' in Japanese. The mould sets to work on a soybean's starches, converting them to fermentable sugars and thus readying them for making into shoyu (soy sauce), sake, miso and other common foods.

The utility of *Aspergillus* is of long provenance. Its earliest literary mention appears in the *Zhouli*, an ancient Chinese text written around 300 BCE. Tombs of estimable personages dating to 165 BCE were discovered to contain soybean koji among the supplies for the trip to the afterworld. And in the *Shiji*, China's most famous historical work written a century later, appears discussion of the stuff as the country's most important commodity. This commodity had found its way west by 1776 in the form of Bowen's Patent Soy, a type of shoyu brewed by its namesake, the American Samuel Bowen, at his headquarters in colonial Georgia.[5]

Shoyu is made today much as it was in Asian antiquity, as are other koji-based foods such as tempeh, sake and miso. And each food is the result of the fascinating transformation worked by *Aspergillus*. The production of shoyu, for instance, involves mixing equal amounts of boiled soybeans and roasted wheat and then inoculating the mixture with a spore culture. The culture depends on the kind of shoyu made. In brewing tamari shoyu, the fungus *Aspergillus tamarii* is introduced to the soybean–wheat mixture, which is then left to ferment. There follows an aminoglycosidic reaction, as it is known. The microbes break down grain proteins into free amino acids and protein fragments, and starches into simple sugars. The result is shoyu's signature brown colour. Lactic acid bacteria then ferment the sugars present in the mixture into lactic acid, and yeast makes ethanol, the ageing of which produces the shoyu's characteristic flavours.

*Aspergillus* works much the same way in the production of tempeh and sake. In tempeh, the mould colonizes boiled soybeans and ferments them into a more digestible food. (Prisoners of war in the Vietnam conflict reportedly owed their survival to tempeh;

they could not digest unfermented soybeans.) In the production of sake, *Aspergillus oryzae* breaks down rice starch, which is resistant to yeast fermentation, into sugars that the yeast converts to ethyl alcohol and carbon dioxide. In this way the Chinese were able to make wines as delicious and intoxicating as anything from the vineyards of France or Austria.

In the 1890s a Japanese chemist named Jokichi Takamine even used koji to make whisky. Takamine's method marked a departure from traditional methods, which typically involved introducing yeast to fruit juice or malted cereal mash for fermentation. A koji starter, on the other hand, Takamine regarded as more economical and efficient, because he found that *A. oryzae* produced more enzymes that degrade starches than did malting, especially when the medium in use was wheat bran. Plus, the fungus itself grew in a mere three days, after which it was ready for harvest. (Barley requires six months.) Takamine also observed that his koji method enabled microorganisms to survive longer in liquids whose alcohol was high and thus contributed to raising the alcohol content higher still.[6]

Takamine's success in the laboratory unfortunately did not translate to success in the marketplace. Consumers who had sampled his koji-based whisky found its flavour strange. Takamine nonetheless showed the way to wider possibility for *Aspergillus* in its impressive versatility. It is used today for making citric acid and enzymes essential to industrial food production.

Yet *Aspergillus* may be as much a bane as a boon. About fifty species of *Aspergillus* produce toxic metabolites. And they infect such foods as nuts, grains and spices.[7] The poisonous species *Aspergillus flavus* grows especially well in tropical and subtropical climates, infecting food to produce deadly aflatoxins that cause acute liver damage, liver cirrhosis and tumours. It has been suggested that the high incidence of liver cancer in central Africa and parts of Southeast Asia owes to the consumption of aflatoxins.[8] In

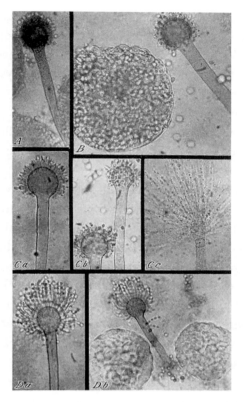

Images of various strains of *Aspergillus*. Certain strains are detrimental, even deadly; others are harmless, even beneficial. Examples of the latter kind are the strains that go into making such familiar Asian foods as soy sauce and tempeh.

1974 some four hundred people in India contracted hepatitis from *A. flavus*-infected corn. Of those affected, 106 died.[9]

The Janus-faced character of *Aspergillus* betokens that of the fungi kingdom generally. Proper understanding and appreciation of the seemingly mysterious role members of this kingdom play in fermenting food require that we know something of their nature and history. A vast and ancient lineage accounts for much of fungi's singularity. Two of the oldest life forms on earth, fungi and bacteria descended from a common ancestor about 550 million years ago.

This head start led to a proliferation into an estimated 100,000 species of fungi and fungus-like organisms. Today, some 5 million fungi are thought to exist.[10] Many assume impressive forms. An article in *Nature* from 1992 relates the genetic analysis of a flush of the fungus *Armillaria gallica* – honey mushroom – in a 35-acre northern Michigan woodland.[11] The fruiting bodies proved to be identical rather than individual. The subsoil mycelium network that produced those bodies was 1,500 years old – one of the oldest living organisms on earth.[12]

Their ancient lineage means fungi played an important role in the evolution of other organisms. For instance, we can thank fungi for the rich variety of plants on earth. Some scientists speculate that a symbiotic relationship between a fungus and a photosynthesizing organism during the Cambrian period some 485 million years ago paved the way for the later rise of plants.[13] This symbiosis has survived into the present. Fungi that grow around roots of vascular plants – mycorrhizae – increase nutrient uptake in some 90 per cent of plant species.[14] The Indian pipe plant common to the northeastern u.s. and elsewhere benefits from such a partnership. On its dense, hard root mass there appear many small, branched, nub-like structures about 3 mm (an eighth of an inch) long and 1 mm (0.04 in.) in diameter. A microscope reveals that each nub is enclosed in a fungal mycelium, the hyphae of which penetrate the root to deliver food to the cells and out into the soil to gather nutrients.[15] The proto-conifers of the Carboniferous age 350 million years ago had an almost identical relationship with a similar fungus.[16]

Although fungi assist plants in ways essential to their survival, they have more in common with humans. Whereas cellulose forms plant cell walls, the building block of fungi cells' walls is the strong, flexible polysaccharide chitin found also in fish scales and the exoskeletons of shellfish and insects.[17] This unique chitin connection situates fungi somewhere between plants and animals.

Fungal hyphae mass. In reproduction, a fungus's fruiting bodies – the portion visible above ground – scatter spores. From spores issue hyphae, which grow and become entangled in a dense network known as a mycelium. Hyphae can be tough and tenacious, establishing themselves in concrete, ship's planks and other unlikely environments.

Their way of feeding is unique as well. Not reliant on sunlight for energy, fungi draw nutriment from decaying matter by secreting enzymes extracellularly to break down complex molecules into simpler forms.[18] When they are ready to reproduce, they do so through spores, which swell like seeds when exposed to moisture. The cell wall of the spore expands through an existing weak spot called a germ pore. This expansion becomes a type of tube – called, fittingly, a 'germ tube' – and this tube in turn becomes a filament known as a hypha. As a hypha grows it begins to branch, becoming many hyphae, elongating in such a way that the cell wall at the growing end of each remains elastic enough for the wall to extend yet rigid enough to keep the protoplasm secured within it and nutrients streaming to other parts of the fungus. Eventually, the hyphae tangle and thicken into a colony. Grown large enough, the colony becomes a 'mycelium'.[19] A mushroom plucked from the forest floor will have fine, trailing strands of the stuff. The plucked part, the fruiting body, is merely the reproductive structure of a much larger organism beneath the soil. Once it reaches a certain maturity it scatters its spores and the growth cycle begins anew.

\* \* \*

In its irrepressibility, fungal life could impoverish farmers even as it enriched cheesemakers and shoyu brewers.

In 1843, some forty years before Emil Hansen would begin his work on isolating pure yeast cultures, one of the most devastating blights in history struck the mid-Atlantic u.s., killing half the potato crop of Pennsylvania and Delaware. The 'new disease' left dark spots along the leaves' margins and covered their undersides with white mycelia bearing sporangia – receptacles in which asexual spores form. The tubers themselves became darkly mottled and later putrid.[20] 'If a man could imagine his own plight, with growths

Potato infected with *Phytophthora infestans*, the microorganism that famously played a central role in the Great Famine in mid-19th-century Ireland.

of some weird and colourless seaweed issuing from his mouth and nostrils, from roots which were destroying and choking both his digestive system and his lungs,' the twentieth-century plant pathologist Ernest Large wrote of the blight, 'he would have a very crude and fabulous, but perhaps instructive idea of the condition of the potato plant when its leaves were mouldy with *Botrytis* [*Phytophthora*] *infestans.*'[21]

By 1844 the blight had reached the U.S. Midwest and into Canada. The British Isles saw its first case during the cool, rainy summer of 1845. The wet weather ensured the blight's rapid spread. Particularly hard hit was Ireland, which lost 40 per cent of the year's potato crop. The following year the loss rocketed to 90 per cent.[22] Subsequent years saw the blight's occasional return. All told, 1 million people died of starvation in its wake.

Though many attributed the blight to everything from divine wrath to electrical influences, one forward-thinking soul sought a likelier explanation. In 1846 the Reverend Miles Joseph Berkeley published an article on the blight in the *Journal of the Horticultural Society of London*. His systematic investigation brought him to the conclusion that the 'decay is the consequence of the presence of the mould, and not the mould of the decay . . . The plant then becomes unhealthy in consequence of the presence of the mould, which feeds upon its juices.'[23] He could confidently claim therefore that the mould was 'the immediate cause of destruction'.[24]

The good reverend's cogent argument for the cause of the potato blight represented a tremendous advance, if only because it showed the relationship between fungi and crop failure to be incontrovertibly real.[25] (It bears mentioning, however, that the potato blight is in fact not a true fungus; it is, rather, a fungus-like microorganism called an oomycete.) Yet it also brought with it sobering insight: 'When a survey is made of the extensive feeding grounds utilized by the fungi, encompassing as they do every corner of the earth, and every form of organic material upon it,' mycologists Robert Thatcher Rolfe and F. W. Rolfe wrote, 'one is immediately struck by the general similarity between their wants and our own.'[26] And for centuries fungi succeeded in satisfying the former at the expense of the latter.

The fungi–blight connection came as an unsettling revelation, laying bare as it had the fragility of human endeavour. Though invisible fungi brought the misery and destruction, hatred and distrust soon extended to the visible kinds. 'Beneath trees and hedgerows the ripe mosses gleamed, and coral and amber fungi, with amanita and other hooded folk,' wrote the British author Eden Phillpotts. 'In companies and clusters they sprang, or arose misshapen, sinister, and alone.'[27] It was guilt by association.

Unlike the unseen threat of bacteria, visible fungi inspired visceral fear, disgust and bewilderment. People wondered whence such strange organisms came. Aristotle's successor Theophrastus, for example, believed that truffles came from thunderstorms and rain. Their mysterious formations bade both good and ill. Greek physician and poet Nicander (c. 185 BCE) called fungi 'evil ferment of the earth',[28] while the Roman naturalist Pliny the Elder (23–79 CE), writing a few centuries later, described truffles as 'the most wonderful of all things' because 'the fruit . . . can spring up and live without a root'.[29] Fungi left their mark on classical art. An Etruscan vase depicts a dying centaur gripping a mushroom between his hooves, his single visible eye noticeably dilated. An Attic vase shows Perseus with mushrooms; another, a priest bearing a trio of mushrooms on a platter as he attends the sacrifice of a pig by Hercules.[30]

The association of mushrooms with such esteemed figures as centaurs and priests meant they were used in ritual and often in medical treatment. One of the most common mushrooms used during this period was the agarikon (*Laricifomes officinalis*). The Greek physician Dioscorides wrote of its properties that it is 'styptic and heat-producing, efficacious against colic and sores, fractured limbs, and bruises from falls'.[31] It also aids in treatment of 'liver complaints, asthma, jaundice, dysentery, kidney disease', as well as stomach pains, epilepsy, menstruation, and 'flatulence in women'.[32] 'On the whole,' Dioscorides concluded, 'it is serviceable in all internal complaints when taken according to the age and strength of the patient.'[33]

Dioscorides evidently had much experience with fungi, and he took care to avoid those he believed poisonous. These grew 'among rusty nails or rotten rags, or near serpents' holes, or on trees producing noxious fruits'.[34] They could be identified by a 'thick coating of mucus' and the fact that when laid aside after gathering they 'quickly become putrid'.[35] Those who consumed fungi heedless of the warnings paid the price.[36] Tales of such unfortunate souls were common. The historian Eparchides wrote about the playwright Euripides, who in 450 BCE was on a visit to Icarus when he learned of the deaths of a woman, her two adult sons and her unwed daughter that had been caused by a meal of mushrooms. The event moved him to pen an epigram to their memory.[37]

Worse still was when the hand of pitiless fate struck invisibly. In antiquity, blights and rusts were considered instances of divine retribution. The Hebrew prophet Amos thundered on behalf of the Almighty, 'I have smitten you with blasting and mildew.'[38] Scholars G. L. Carefoot and E. R. Sprott have linked rusts to Pharaoh's dream of 'seven thin ears' in Genesis 41:7, the image foretelling a grain blight in the southern Levant that would force the Jews into Egypt and eventual enslavement.[39] The Romans likewise saw unseen powers at work whenever rusts destroyed their crops. Annual spring festivals in the seventh century BCE existed to propitiate the rust god Robigus. A procession would leave Rome by the Flaminian gate, cross the Milvian bridge and proceed to the fifth milestone on the Claudian Way. There, in a sacred grove, prayers would precede the sacrifice of a dog, always reddish, and a sheep.[40] This, the Romans hoped, would move the god to spare their crops.

Even if Robigus spared them, Romans had other mycological dangers to their crops to fear. The fungus ergot, for one, terrorized communities well into the twentieth century. Appearing as a black, crescent-shaped malignancy on ears of rye, ergot contains high amounts of complex organic compounds called ergoline alkaloids. Once ingested, these compounds begin to wreak havoc on smooth muscle tissue and the nervous system, causing symptoms that range from a burning sensation in the limbs to hallucinations and convulsions.[41] In 857 CE the first recorded account of ergotism came from the Lower Rhenish settlement of Kanten. Villagers were described as having suffered from swollen blisters, and some reportedly had arms and legs fall off. About a century later an outbreak in Paris was recorded, with victims describing a sensation of fire in the limbs. Indeed, ergot outbreaks happened regularly in the Middle Ages. The symptoms of ergotism came to be associated with St Anthony. Sufferers made pilgrimages to reliquaries of his in Europe, and the houses of the Order of St Anthony had red-painted walls as a symbol of the disease. 'St Anthony's Fire', as the condition was called, even influenced history. In 1722 the Turkish army defeated Russian tsar Peter the Great's forces. Blame for the loss fell on a supply of bread that had become contaminated by ergot and sickened the cavalry troops. They suffered convulsions, and flesh from their hands and feet sloughed off as if injured by frostbite.[42]

As wheat, which better resists contamination, began to replace rye as a staple grain and awareness of ergot and its effects grew, incidents of ergotism declined. People learned that in fact ergot had its uses. In the Middle Ages midwives gave small doses of it to expectant mothers in order to induce contractions and speed childbirth. And it is used today to relieve migraine headaches.[43]

Like bacteria, fungi revealed themselves as Janus-faced, neither wholly evil nor wholly benign in nature. Appreciation of this nature informed their study. In 1601 the French botanist Carolus

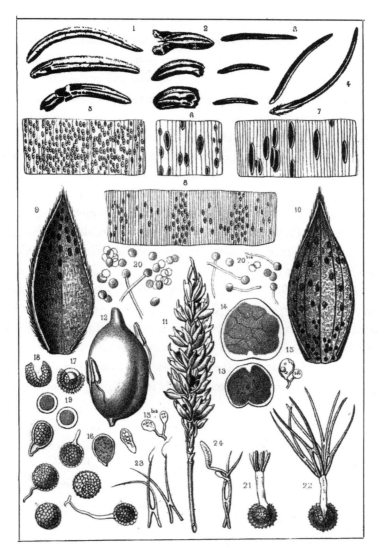

Schematic rendering of various grains susceptible to infection by ergot smut. Ingestion of affected grain bred a host of dire symptoms, the most alarming of which was the loss of skin on the hands and feet. As rye ceded to wheat – a smut-resistant grain – as a staple crop, outbreaks of ergotism began to decline.

Clusius taxonomized fungi for the first time, dividing them into two classes, edible and poisonous. His represented a pioneering attempt at fathoming the relationship between fungi and disease. Though this goal would be met, slow, often uncertain means of communication meant slow, often uncertain progress towards it. Many thinkers failed to get it right: they saw fungi as the result of disease rather than its cause. (This belief prevailed until the final quarter of the eighteenth century.) Blame for blight also continued to fall on meteors, animals and pests. Erroneous thinking on the matter persisted because the culprits had invisibility on their side. Not until Dutch merchant Antonie van Leeuwenhoek first observed with his handmade microscopes the budding of yeasts did scientists begin to understand the organisms that caused so much trouble in the visible world.

Robert Hooke – scientist, architect, Royal Society councilman and curator of experiments, Gresham Professor of Geometry, surveyor to the City of London – described the world of microfungi, which he investigated with a compound microscope of his own design and construction. 'The Blue and White and several kinds of hairy mouldy spots,' he wrote of mould in his *Micrographia* of 1665,

> which are observable upon divers kinds of *putrify'd* bodies, whether Animal substances or Vegetable ... are all of them nothing else but several kinds of small and variously figur'd Mushrooms, which, from convenient materials in those *putrifying* bodies, are ... excited to a certain kind of vegetation.[44]

So compelling were Hooke's descriptions that the famous British diarist Samuel Pepys praised *Micrographia* as 'the most ingenious book I ever read in my life' and claimed it kept him awake until the early hours of the morning.[45] Hooke's book contained the first drawings of microfungi, including elegant illustrations of *Mucor* and *Phragmidium mucronatum*, or rose rust. Hooke was also the

Hooke's rendering of the *Mucor* microfungus as it appears in his *Micrographia* (1665). Though his pioneering investigations made visible a previously invisible domain of life, Hooke offered only the haziest conjecture on microfungal reproduction.

first to give an account of the internal structure of mushrooms. Their origins, however, remained a mystery to him. He wrote that he could not see how 'mushrooms may be generated from a seed'. Rather, they 'seem to depend upon a convenient constitution of the matter out of which they are made, and a concurrence of either natural or artificial heat'.[46]

A century later, a sickly bureaucrat named Agostino Bassi would come closer to understanding not only how fungi reproduce, but how they blight their hosts as they do so. Born in 1773 in Italy's Lombardy region, Bassi became an official under the Napoleonic regime. Though he likely would have wished to remain in this comfortable office, poor health and eyesight forced him to resign. He went to live on his father's farm in Mairago, where he devoted himself to things agricultural and scientific, writing a 460-page book on sheep farming, among other pursuits. Early in life he had developed an interest in the muscardine disease of silkworms, which had rocked the silk industries of Italy and France. He would pursue this interest over the course of his life, conducting strange and often baroque experiments on silkworms, 'subjecting them even to the most barbarous treatment', he wrote, going on to note that 'the poor creatures died by thousands and in a thousand ways.' One of these ways involved enclosing the silkworms in a paper bag that he hung in a chimney over a continuous fire. The dried remains he then stored in a cellar. This treatment produced what looked like muscardine disease, albeit without the 'contagious faculty'. This failure left the sensitive Italian 'humiliated in the extreme, silent and idle', and 'oppressed by a terrible melancholy'.[47]

The spell of torpor proved short-lived. With renewed determination and a fresh idea Bassi resumed his experiments. The idea was controversial: muscardine did not happen spontaneously, as was thought at the time; rather, it arrived from an 'extraneous germ'. Bassi looked again at the white efflorescence that covered diseased silkworms. This, he thought, might be the culprit. He examined it with his compound microscope, which was of the same design as Hooke's own, and saw 'a plant of the cryptogamic kind, a parasitic fungus'. A series of experiments showed Bassi's theory to be correct; the disease spread from worm to worm when the fungus spread over the surface of the dead, and every outbreak 'could be traced to the introduction of infected silkworms or the use of contaminated cages or utensils'.[48]

Bassi had identified fungi as the agents of disease. In 1834 he experimentally replicated his findings before a commission of nine professors of medicine and philosophy at the Imperial Royal University of Pavia. Though a few members expressed reservations, the commission found the experiment's results convincing. Doubts notwithstanding, Bassi forged ahead, turning his attention to diseases of mulberry, vine and potato.[49] Around the same time in England, zoologist Richard Owen dissected a dead flamingo at the London Zoo. Mould coated the bird's lungs. Owen thus concluded that entophytic fungus caused the bird's demise. In Paris David Gruby – physician to Dumas *père* and *fils*, Liszt, Chopin and George Sand – identified the fungal nature of ringworm, thrush and other human ailments.[50] Experiments of this nature were being done throughout Europe, and they all ended in a single inevitable insight: fungus caused disease in plants, animals and human beings.

Scientists had finally established that these microorganisms came in various forms and did various harm. They had yet to establish, however, how they managed to do so. Information on this latter concern was slow to arrive. Until the beginning of the nineteenth century, almost all publications on fungi were of European origin – French and German especially.[51] A shift to the English-speaking world would not happen until the twentieth century, which also saw mycology – the study of fungi – emerge as an academic discipline. (It bears adding that, like astronomy, mycology has always invited contributions from amateurs; indeed, its advancement depended on them, as it did also on the founding of mycological societies.) This late development may explain why, relative to their numbers, few fungi have been identified, and even fewer have been studied for possible benefit to human health or diet. The fungal world remains for the most part as alien as it is vast.

Alien, vast – and absolutely indispensable. Without aid from the fungal kingdom our own would be quite a poor one indeed. Yet if one lesson is remembered from this brief history of fungi, it is that we must alloy our appreciation of it with caution. Scientific and medical literature abounds with instances of fungi's sometimes dicey duality and its effects. The many moulds belonging to the genus *Penicillium*, for example, represent one such mixed bag, some figuring in the creation of delectable cheeses and others causing liver, kidney and brain damage.

Just as fraught as ingesting the wrong kind of fungus is ingesting too much of an otherwise right kind. The yeast *Candida kefyr* produces the tart, fizzy dairy drink so popular these days, but it also has it dangers. One expectant mother who overdid it on dairy products, often drinking kefir and eating yoghurt and raw cheese three times daily, gave her twin foetuses an acute fungal infection.[52] And an avid Australian home brewer fell deathly ill when one of the moulds essential for making tempeh, *Rhizopus oryzae*, found its way into a batch of his beer and, by way of this, his small intestine.[53] Though such cases rarely occur, that they occur at all ought to be cause enough for exercising prudence and care when working with fungi. (This warning applies especially to anyone who is immunocompromised.)

Now that we have lingered over this note of caution, we can hurry on to consideration of another microorganism essential to the production of fermented foods: bacteria.

# 5 One of the Miracles
of Everyday Life:
*The Origins, Power and
Fortunes of Vegetable Ferments*

The judge of the assize court too, though he can scarcely, in
fairness, be spoken of as a thorough boor, revels between the
intervals of his judicial duties (like Cincinnatus of old) in the
richness of his manure, rather than the subtleties of jurisprudence; and is prone, when he lays aside the sword of justice, to
wield the cabbage-slicer instead, for the due preparation of his
winter stock of *Sauer-kraut*.
– Henry Mayhew, *German Life and Manners as Seen in Saxony
at the Present Day* (1864)[1]

FROM AGRICULTURE'S BIRTH in the Neolithic Age to the early
twentieth century, the human diet had as its pillars bread and
alcoholic drink. The rich hoarded and traded them, and those
who were not rich relied utterly on them for most of their caloric
intake. Bread was indeed the staff of life – and alcohol a means of
forgetting just how tough hoisting that staff could be.

Yet men and women did not live on bread and beer alone.
They sometimes dressed up otherwise bland meals with more
nutritious foods – vegetables, dairy and, every so often, meat. These
highly perishable foods required careful preservation if they were

to make it to the table. Fermentation offered a ready means of doing so. A hedge against an uncertain future, a looking ahead, it eased any present anxiety. Every culture engaged in this work, creating countless varieties of fermented foods, each one as unique as its place of origin. These ferments gained in importance over time, going from village staple to fuel for crossing continents and sailing the high seas. Like grain and alcohol, they were imported and exported, sold near and far, albeit not without difficulty at times. And they stood as a testament to human ingenuity and a wisdom born from centuries of observation. Though they could not explain why, people knew fermented foods brought health and their absence sickness. They were, in short, one of the miracles of everyday life.

* * *

In 1768 explorer and British navy captain James Cook issued an order that every one of his crew members was to eat 2 lb (*c.* 900 g) of sauerkraut weekly. The sailors did not greet this command happily; they knew sauerkraut as a Dutch food, and as such it seldom appeared on British plates. Full compliance came when Cook's sailors observed his most highly decorated officers eating their rations of sauerkraut with apparent relish. Only then did his sailors come around to the dish they had deemed unpalatable. They even came to regard it as 'the finest stuff in the world'.[2]

Cook did not simply wish to foist alien cuisine on his sailors. Method lay behind his apparent madness for fermented cabbage. Each ration supplied about 150 mg of ascorbic acid. When supplemented with vinegar, mustard and concentrated orange and lemon juices, this serving of fermented cabbage kept away scurvy, a painful scourge of sailors for centuries. In 1519 Portuguese explorer Ferdinand Magellan set sail with three ships and two hundred sailors. Three years and one trip around the globe later, one ship and eighteen men remained. Scurvy had killed most of the rest.

James Gillray, *Germans Eating Sour-Krout*, 1803, etching. Though fondness for fermented cabbage among people of central Europe and the Low Countries may have struck the British as strange, they soon learned to appreciate the dish for its potent nutritional properties.

Scurvy stood as perhaps the most acute symptom of a larger deficiency: a meagre diet. Magellan's men subsisted on biscuit crumbs and tainted water. And their experience evidently did little to instruct future generations of seafarers. Salted beef, pork and fish, beer, rum, flour, dried peas and oats, cheese, butter, molasses and hardtack cakes – such were the foods that were loaded aboard eighteenth-century English ships before a long voyage. They were, in fact, the standard fare of sailors throughout the Western world. Though the Dutch may have eaten more lard and sauerkraut and the Spanish more oil and pickled vegetables, the fundamentals remained the same: starch, protein and precious little in the way of foods that provide vitamin C.[3] To make matters worse, these stores rotted in short order. Hardtack and salted meats grew mould and teemed with maggots. Cheese grew fetid or so hard that sailors carved pieces from it to use as buttons. And beer and water soured. What little nutrition these foods might have contained was destroyed even before they could be eaten.

It only took a few weeks for the effects of such a diet to tell on a sailor. His gums might become swollen and an angry red, his breath foul. He might feel listless and despondent. Dark blotches might break out all over him, and the tissue of his limbs might begin to die. All were signs of scurvy. 'It rotted all my gums, which gave out black and putrid blood,' wrote one English ship's surgeon.

> My thighs and lower legs were black and gangrenous, and I
> was forced to use my knife each day to cut into the flesh in
> order to release this black and foul blood. I also used my knife
> on my gums, which were livid and growing over my teeth.[4]

Remedies as drastic as those described by the unfortunate surgeon became unnecessary in time, thanks to the discovery of vitamin C's preventive powers. As it happened, sauerkraut did not have a particularly high amount of the vitamin. It did have enough, however, for keeping symptoms of scurvy in check, especially when other foods accompanied it. Yet sauerkraut did have a second virtue to recommend it: it was usually the last of a voyage's food stores to spoil, because its manner of preparation, lactic acid fermentation, preserved it. A daily dose of this tangy, probiotic-rich food kept Cook's sailors healthy enough to explore – and, sadly, exploit – distant lands.

Cook's sauerkraut rations epitomized the small yet important role played by fermented fruits and vegetables in widening the range and scale of human activity, from seafaring in search of trade (or plunder) to waging war and building empires. But they had long historical precedent. The builders of the Great Wall of China in the third century BCE kept hale enough to work by eating lactic acid bacteria-fermented vegetables. Roman soldiers grew vegetables in whatever lands they conquered, and much of

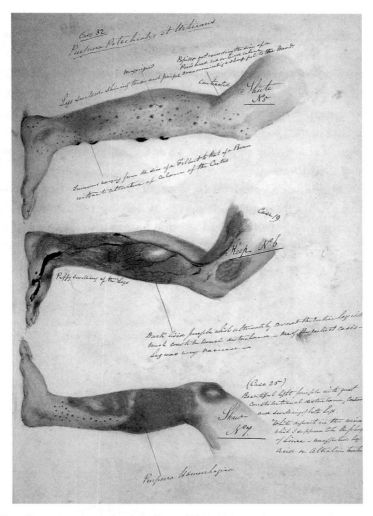

The effects of scurvy, as drawn by Henry Walsh Mahon in his journal, c. 1840. A disease brought on by a deficiency of vitamin C, scurvy continued to plague British sailors until it began to be better understood. Part of that understanding included the preventive powers of sauerkraut, a dish unfamiliar to British palates. Its levels of ascorbic acid were sufficiently high to keep symptoms at bay.

this produce they likely pickled. Although the vital nutritional importance of vitamin C only became known in the 1930s following the Hungarian chemist Albert Szent-Györgyi's discovery of ascorbic acid and its role in human metabolism, fermented fruits and vegetables had long been valued as a hedge against want. Association with the divine, a cultural tendency common to staple foods, extended to them. Pre-Christian Lithuanians, for example, included among their pantheon a god of pickles and beer whom they called Roguszys.[5]

Despite such colourful folklore, no god made these foods. Their seemingly miraculous power of defying spoilage owes to the action of some of the world's humblest creatures. Plant matter from oak leaves to cucumbers has living on it lactic acid bacteria

Albert Szent-Györgyi, Hungarian chemist who discovered the role of vitamin C in human metabolism and nutrition. Fermenting cabbage into sauerkraut had long served as a solution for storage. It has also been found to render ascorbic acid more bioavailable than it is in the raw product.

that, whenever brined, immersed in a pickling solution or left to ferment in some other way, acidify that medium as an effect of their reproduction. (Yoghurt, for example, may be made by immersing pepper stems in milk.) Lactic acid bacteria are Gram-positive (possessed of a thick, multilayer sheet of the polymer peptidoglycan), facultative anaerobic (able to live without oxygen), non-sporulating, non-motile, acid tolerant, and usually rod-shaped, though they can also be round. The acid they produce inhibits the growth of other, potentially more dangerous bacteria.[6] They prefer habitats rich in minerals and carbohydrates, hence their presence in wine, beer and vegetable and dairy ferments. Yet they also have a diverse metabolic capacity: they can live almost anywhere and under almost any conditions – extreme cold, for example, as well as long storage. They are often found on plants and in human and animals' bodies. This tremendous hardiness is why they ferment food so successfully.[7]

The way in which microorganisms produce these foods depends on whether they are homofermentative or heterofermentative, designations that have nothing to do with sexual preference. Rather, they refer to the by-products a microorganism produces when it ferments carbohydrates. Homofermentative bacteria feed on glucose and leave lactic acid as their primary by-product. Such bacteria are often used in dairy starters to produce yoghurt and cheese.[8] Heterofermentative bacteria feed on glucose and leave lactic acid, ethanol, acetic acid and carbon dioxide. The by-product left by any one kind of heterofermentative bacteria is unpredictable. For this reason they do not appear in many controlled ferments. Such bacteria cause cheese to develop cracks and fissures and yoghurt packaging to bloat with gas. Sometimes lactic acid bacteria produce gas from other substances, such as citrate, gluconate and certain amino acids. When properly controlled these may impart flavour and other desirable qualities to buttermilk, sour cream and cultured butter. When uncontrolled they may spoil a ferment.[9]

Under ideal conditions lactic acid fermentation is akin to a well-scripted play. No one kind of bacteria dominates. As the ferment progresses, a cast of bacterial characters play particular roles, each lending a unique flavour or odour to the pleasing complexity of the whole. Take Cook's beloved sauerkraut, for example. In the opening act, in which the cabbage is first packed tightly into barrels, aerobic bacteria claim the spotlight, supported by a host of bit players in the form of other microorganisms present in the cabbage and water. They combine to ferment into lactic, acetic, formic and succinic acids, causing the liquid to bubble and foam. Activity increases. Meanwhile, the pH decreases.

Then, the next act: heterofermentative lactic acid bacteria appear, causing the lactic acid concentration to rise to 1 per cent. Lured by the lack of oxygen, the abundant salt and the low pH, the homofermentative lactic acid bacteria take the stage. The lactic acid rises to 1.5 to 2.0 per cent. Finally – and this only happens with sauerkraut aged in barrels, such as may be found in a delicatessen – *Lactobacillus brevis* usher in the final act, along with some heterofermentative bacteria that feed on pentoses (monosaccharides with five carbon atoms) released by the breakdown of cell walls. The acid content now rises to 2.5 per cent, and the curtain falls on a sauerkraut rich in complexity.[10]

Acidification renders the medium inhospitable to food-borne pathogenic bacteria and other undesirable microorganisms. The lactic acid bacteria cease reproducing once the medium has become too acidic for them to continue. During the final stage of fermentation lactic acid bacteria and other acid-tolerant bacteria dominate the solution, and this maintains the shelf-stability of the vegetable ferment.[11]

The straightforward and rather unvarying process of vegetable fermentation belies the great variety it admits of. Like all fermentation, it depends on intricate interactions among microorganisms, environmental conditions, the matter fermented and sundry other

particulars. Any vegetable ferment's character thus takes on something of the character of its place of preparation. A recipe native to
one locale may be shared or adapted to suit the demands of another.
Sauerkraut, for example, did not remain a peculiarly Dutch food
once it had found its way on to Captain Cook's ships. (In fact,
sauerkraut was not a peculiarly Dutch food at all; it likely originated
with the Mongols of northern China.) Once sauerkraut became
more familiar to the British, they began adapting it to their tastes
by adding apples and pears, as well as dill, oak and cherry leaves.
Germans preferred a sauerkraut amply flecked with caraway seeds,
and Poles, who according to lore got their recipe from the Tatars,
delighted in the addition of wild mushrooms.

Yet commonalities among ferments, especially in their production, can also be found. Strikingly similar techniques for making
sauerkraut are shared in regions otherwise separated by vast distances and time. Pit fermentation stands as one example. In Cook's
day, brined cabbage fermented in barrels or special wood-lined pits,
a method of large-scale sauerkraut production rare in present-day
Europe but alive and well in the South Pacific.[12] Islanders first
dig a pit and line it with banana leaves as protection against soil
contamination. In the pit they place cleaned and dried pieces of
starchy fruits and vegetables such as banana, plantain, cassava,
breadfruit, taro, sweet potato, arrowroot and yam. They place more
banana leaves over the full pit, and over the leaves, stones. The
pit's contents ferment over the ensuing three to six weeks, after
which time the Islanders remove it for macerating and drying
in the sun. (The stuff fresh from the pit reportedly has a strong
smell owing to the presence of propionic acid, which also gives
Swiss cheese its distinctive odour.) Only after cooking, the final
act of this laborious process, is the fermented stuff considered fit
for long-term storage.[13]

Pit fermentation remains alive not only in remote islands of
the Pacific; it survives among the highest peaks of Asia, as well.

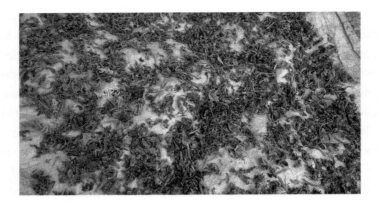

Gundruk made from cauliflower leaves. A product of pit fermentation, which imparts to the greens used a pleasant tang, gundruk owes its status as a Nepalese dietary mainstay to its flavour, portability and storability.

Himalayan peoples use it to make a ferment of leafy greens called *gundruk*. How they came to do so is the stuff of legend. Farmers of ancient Nepal would sometimes have to flee their villages when war threatened. The crops of rice and green leafy vegetables they left behind could rot in the field or fall to invaders. A ruler whose name has gone unrecorded by history hit on an idea for hedging against either eventuality. He would have farmers somehow create stores of preserved vegetables that were invisible to invaders. They set about in execution of his plan, digging pits, filling them with harvested rice and radish roots, and covering the pits with hay and mud. Whenever any threat of war receded or marauders had moved on, they returned to empty the pits. Though the rice had become unpleasant smelling, the vegetables had taken on a pleasantly acidic taste. Dried in the sun for a few days, they tasted even better, especially when added to pickles and soups. So well had the vegetables been preserved, in fact, that they stored and travelled well – perfect for journeys or the long Himalayan monsoon season – and thus gundruk became a staple of the Nepalese diet.[14]

\* \* \*

Any vegetable fermentation that requires a shovel can be, well, the pits. Fortunately, cultures throughout the world found ways that required no holes in the ground. Another method of ancient origin, vessel fermentation, remains in practice today. It is how kimchi, a popular Korean lactic acid vegetable ferment, has been made for centuries. Documents from Korea's later Silla dynasty (668–935 CE) list stone pickle jars among the items needed for vegetable fermentation in the Bupju temple, near Mount Sokri.[15] And the first explicit mention of kimchi appears in written records that date to the middle years of the Koryŏ dynasty (935–1392 CE). 'Preserved in soybean paste kimchi tastes good in summer,' writes a poet of the period, 'whereas kimchi pickled in brine is served as a good side dish during the winter.'[16] The garlic and red pepper in the brine kept evil spirits away, Koreans believed, which at any rate is something they did to harmful microorganisms. Ginger, tangerine peel, melon and pear could also garnish a ferment.

Seasons not only influenced the kind of kimchi that tasted best, as the poet noted; they affected kimchi's making and storage as well. Kimchi only kept for a few days in summer, traditionally the season of its production. To preserve it for longer, people lowered it down wells or buried stone jars of it in the earth. Spared spoilage in hot weather by these methods of storage, it kept throughout winter when fresh cabbage could not be had. Yet kimchi was no mere ration for lean times. In fermentation it developed flavours so appealing that it became a favourite condiment. To this day Koreans eat kimchi with nearly every meal.

Kimchi's counterpart in the West was olives. And like kimchi, the practice of fermenting olives in vessels reached into antiquity. Cultivation of olive trees for their fruit dates to the twelfth millennium BCE. It began in Asia Minor and in time spread to Syria, Greece, parts of Africa (Egypt, Nubia, Ethiopia, the Atlas Mountains) and parts of Europe. The Romans aided this dissemination, for as they did with their beloved grapevines, they

Museum miniature display depicting the traditional preparation of kimchi. Perhaps the most iconic of all Korean dishes, kimchi has been developed into a host of varieties. An easily stored ferment, it offered security against lean times. Yet its many gustatory virtues also recommend it to the most refined palates.

introduced olive trees wherever climate and conditions allowed.[17] The agriculturalist and writer Columella, who lived in the first century CE, crowned the olive 'queen of all trees' for its virtue of yielding much fruit with little care.

Columella was not mistaken. The olive tree's easy plenty made its fruit ideal for trade. Earthen jars filled with olive stones have been discovered in sunken Roman ships. Yet the olive tree did put its growers to a bit of trouble: its fruit is unfit to eat until it is fermented. Fermentation removes oleuropein, the chemical responsible for olives' characteristic bitterness. The process involves immersing washed ripe olives in a brine of 5 to 7.5 per cent salt. (Fermentation of unripe olives was rare because their bitterness could only be removed by lye, a chemical not widely available before the nineteenth century.) With time this brine becomes colonized by a number of microorganisms, including yeast. As the brine pulls water from the olives more salt is added. The salt, along with the anaerobic conditions, serves to limit the number of micro-organisms that would otherwise compete with lactic acid bacteria for the olives' sugars. Bacterial metabolism of the sugars makes the brine even more hostile to undesirable microorganisms by lowering its pH. In this, bacteria find help in the olives' oleuropein, which has antimicrobial properties. (The slightly bitter yet fruity flavour characteristic of Greek, Turkish and North African olives owes to residual traces of oleuropein.[18]) Fermentation continues

Illustration, from a 19th-century German textbook, of an olive tree's leaves, flowers and branches. Olives are remarkable in that they require fermentation in order to become edible. Doing so was worth the effort; olives proved to be as versatile as they were flavourful, and they were easy to grow.

until there remains only *Lactobacillus plantarum* and *Lactobacillus delbrueckii*. In this final stage yeasts also infiltrate the ferment, imparting, if in the right amounts, appealing organoleptic qualities. Excessive amounts, however, cause olives to bloat, brine to cloud, and unpleasant flavours and smells to develop. The delicate balance between just enough yeast and too much demands careful monitoring lest a batch should spoil.[19]

Fermentation – its causes, actions and effects – must have seemed miraculous to individuals of eras lacking generally in scientific understanding. More miraculous must it have seemed when fermentation rendered plants edible and nutritious. Even today, in many parts of the world this kind of fermentation means the difference between feast and famine. Cassava is a fine example. A root of a shrub-like plant that grows in Africa and Southeast Asia and the foundation of many diets for both people and animals, it appears in porridges, breads and other staple foods. As it happens, raw cassava is highly toxic. Yet correct handling and preparation transform it into reliable sustenance. And those who rely on it follow the process of removing the root's fibrous outer layer and chopping its starchy inner flesh into bits. They pack the bits in sacks, which they suspend and weight to wring out liquid. As the cassava hangs lactic acid bacteria colonize it, the ensuing fermentation neutralizing the naturally occurring cyanide. Adequately fermented cassava is then grated, sun-dried and, finally, dry-roasted.[20] The end product is used in everything from cake and bread to savoury fritters. Of course, methods varied by region. 'Each of them carried a long cane basket, a machete for cutting down the soft cassava stem, and a little hoe for digging out the tuber,' wrote novelist Chinua Achebe of the method traditional in his native Nigeria in his novel of 1958 *Things Fall Apart*. 'When they had harvested a sizable heap they carried it down in two trips to the stream, where every woman had a shallow well for fermenting her cassava.'[21]

Women peeling cassava tubers. A staple food in parts of Africa, cassava must be submitted to fermentation before it is eaten. Raw it is toxic, owing to naturally occurring cyanide.

The Sudanese employ a method similar to the one described by Achebe in preparing the sicklepod legume (*Senna obtusifolia*), which, like cassava, is naturally toxic. They pound the leaves to a paste, pack the paste in earthenware vessels, cover the vessels in sorghum leaves and bury them in cool, shaded ground. There they leave them to ferment for about two weeks, stirring their contents every three days. They then shape the finished paste into balls some 3 to 6 cm (1.2 to 2.4 in.) around, which they dry in the sun in preparation for storage. The sicklepod-leaf paste, called *kawal*, has a strong odour that often lingers on its handlers. 'When you eat it with your right hand,' a saying goes, 'you smell it on your left.' This proves only a slight nuisance; for all the paste's stench, its pungent flavour enlivens otherwise bland soups, stews and dishes.[22]

Humanity's genius for fermentation encompasses nearly every kind of fruit and vegetable. And this genius was and, in many parts of the world, still is largely domestic in nature. Fermenting went on mostly in the homes of local producers. This was because the process required careful attention and intuitive knowledge; because the vessels, usually stone or earthen, did not lend themselves to easy transport; and because the vessels' contents spoiled or became imbalanced easily. Moreover, the humble scope of the practice suggested something of the lives of its practitioners. Ferments made in age-old ways bespoke people who were largely sedentary and peaceful, or, at the very least, victim to few upheavals.

That vegetable ferments, like many other foods, would later become subject to standardized, large-scale production likewise bespoke of people who were wide-ranging in their movement and expansionist in their aims. In short, they sought to explore, wage war, conquer and occupy. They required, then, ferments stable enough to accompany them on adventures far from home.

\* \* \*

In 1800 Napoleon Bonaparte had his mind set on the conquest of Europe. Among the countless practical considerations in meeting this grand goal was that of feeding the sailors of his navy. He was after meat and vegetables, and he offered 1,200 francs to whomever could devise a way of preparing stores of these foods that would keep at sea. A French chef by the name of Nicolas Appert answered the great general's challenge with a bold solution. He commissioned the blowing of glass bottles of various sizes ranging from those which could accommodate a measure of fruit juice to those which could hold an entire sheep, boiled. He stopped the bottles with cork, and they did the trick. Their contents did not spoil. After claiming his prize Appert went on to publish *The Art of Preserving All Kinds of Animal and Vegetable Substances* in 1811. It was the first cookbook to take up the subject of food preservation methods.

Appert's solution created problems of its own. Although glass bottles did preserve food well, they were fragile and heavy and thus did not lend themselves to easy storage or transport over rough roads and seas. The English inventor Peter Durand came along shortly after Appert with his own solution. He preserved Appert's method but used tin instead of glass. Thus canning was born. It would see further improvements in the mid-nineteenth century with the American Civil War. Before long, canned food went from a soldier's ration to a harried housewife's convenience. Eventually, an ordinary household would likely have had as many cans on its pantry shelves as it would have had Mason jars.

As so often happens, industry sought to capitalize in peace-time on technological advances made by the military in time of war. Between 1870 and 1910, large corporations moved to bring the system of growing, producing and selling food in the United States under their control. One such interest was the H. J. Heinz Company. Founded in 1869 near Pittsburgh, Pennsylvania, it sought to exploit a newfangled method of packing vegetables in

Example of the bottle developed by Nicolas Appert for preserving food over long periods and journeys. Though the bottles worked, winning for Appert the cash prize offered by his emperor, Napoleon Bonaparte, their size, weight and fragility showed them to be ultimately impractical.

jars under steam, which removed the need for boiling the jars in water. The leadership at Heinz saw at once the economic advantage promised by this method: greater quantities of many different fruits and vegetables could be preserved and shipped to market at once. (Something of this advantage is reflected in the '57 varieties' slogan on Heinz labels.) The company further devised methods for peeling, slicing and brining – all work once performed by mothers, grandmothers, grandfathers and other household members. Fermented fruits and vegetables had emerged fully into an era of mass production. By 1910 the industry employed more than 68,000 people and produced some 3 billion cans of food.[23]

With mass production of fermented fruits and vegetables came the need for touting their availability. Mass marketing, itself a young yet burgeoning trade, was something Heinz eagerly availed itself of. The tricks of the trade deployed to induce consumers, mostly female, to forsake their domestic knowledge and skill for ease and convenience were the usual ones of ostentation and giveaways. The 1893 World's Fair in Chicago included a display by Heinz. Fairgoers could drop by to sample the company's many offerings, and representatives would reward them for their troubles with a charm in the form of a small green pickle, the company's logo. The charm could be attached to a bracelet or key ring as a constant reminder of the virtues of canned vegetables. Not that the recipients lacked reminders enough in the wider world; electric signs emblazoned with the Heinz name adorned many a downtown – brilliant triggers for memories of fine factory-made foods.[24]

Heinz executives also understood that transparency won trust. To show that their operations were all sweetness and light, they invited the public to tour their factories. 'The first impression one gets in the Heinz company's workrooms are of a diet kitchen in a hospital, with a host of pretty nurses making dainties for the sick,' reads an account of one such visit in an issue of *Public Hygiene* from 1911.

> A detailed description is not necessary, because the hospital standard of cleanliness and hygiene is everywhere apparent. A physician can readily see how that would work out with 'fifty-seven different kinds'.[25]

The impression the company wished to make was clear: only the Heinz factory could produce pickles guaranteed to be free of harmful germs.

As it had with bread and beer, the hygiene movement convinced the public of the greater safety of vegetables canned in factories. And the factories that canned them did nothing to discourage this impression. Indeed, they both promoted and benefited from the air of scientific and medical legitimacy that had accrued to them. Consumers had come to prefer uniformity and asepsis, which Heinz and its ilk could present their operations – or, at least, carefully stage-managed simulacra of their operations – as delivering. Individuals who continued to ferment vegetables on their own, meanwhile, began to take greater care in bringing

A trade card depicting pickle-making at Heinz. The company pioneered the making of vegetable preserves on an industrial scale. And it touted the clinical cleanliness of its operations, which was sometimes more apparent than real.

their home kitchens up to a similar standard. Guiding them in this were home economics texts such as *Everywoman's Canning Book*. Published in 1918, it warned readers that every 'piece of fruit or vegetable, no matter how fresh, will have on its surface tiny, invisible microorganisms'.[26] It was a home fermenter's duty to wage war on these microscopic enemies.

Lost in the discourse of hygiene had been, of course, that home fermenters already had allies in this war, and that these allies too were microorganisms. The whole art of fermenting came down to marshalling friendly forces against hostile legions. Now undone by imperfectly understood microbiology of the time, this art began to lose adherents, despite many centuries of prior success.

# 6 Microbes Working Their Magic: *Cheese, Yoghurt and Other Dairy Ferments*

i said to myself
if a swiss cheese
could think
it would think that
a swiss cheese
was the most important
thing in the world
just as everything that
can think at all
does think about itself.
– Don Marquis, *Archygrams* (1927)[1]

SHIFTS IN CONSUMER PREFERENCES spurred by the hygiene movement came to influence milk production and consumption as much as they had factory-produced fermented fruits and vegetables. In 1886, the value proposition that had served industrial food interests so well – namely, that they alone could bring clean, safe food to market – would come to apply to milk. That year German agricultural chemist Franz Ritter von Soxhlet devised a process, which he based on Pasteur's theories, for treating this most perishable animal product. He heated milk to 60°C (140°F) for twenty to thirty minutes before pouring it into sterile containers to cool. This ensured the milk was not only safe to drink, but also kept longer and could therefore be transported greater distances.[2] Soxhlet's was admittedly a delicate process, demanding care and exactitude. A higher temperature would destroy the milk's pleasant taste and mouthfeel; a lower would have failed to destroy all the harmful microbes in it.

Soxhlet's success freed milk from its traditional markets – wealthy individuals, whose money enabled them to bear the expense of bringing fresh milk to table; and peasants, whose proximity to the source meant fresh milk was no expense at all – and put it in reach of a new consumer: urban dwellers of modest means, whose lack of access to land and dairy cattle made it a comparative luxury.

Yet those same people often had access to fermented dairy in the form of cheese and butter. Indeed, methods of rendering milk a more stable and portable food had been practised for centuries. Fermentation made milk, a highly perishable food, more stable and portable. And milk lent itself naturally to this transformation. Like fresh vegetables, it harboured untold numbers of microorganisms. *Lactobacillus casei*, *Lactobacillus bulgaricus* and other benign bacteria found its mixture of fat globules, protein, sugars, salts, carbohydrates, minerals, enzymes and water eminently hospitable. (Unfortunately, so too did *Listeria monocytogenes*, tuberculosis bacilli and other infectious microbes; what a bowl of yoghurt or wheel of cheese harboured within it was anyone's guess.) These microbes allowed people to transform highly perishable milk into any number of long-lasting and nutritious dairy products.

This transformation happened by one of three kinds of dairy ferment: lactic, yeast-lactic and fungal-lactic. The first category is typified by such foods as yoghurt and acidophilus milk. Foods of the second kind – kefir, viili and koumiss, for example – evidenced their dependence on bacteria and yeast for fermenting by their effervescence or, in the case of viili, a fuzzy white surface. Cheese belongs solidly to the third kind. Mould-stippled wheels of Roquefort stand as a prime example of fungus working together with bacteria to produce a well-preserved, tasty food. The common denominator in all these ferments is lactic acid bacteria which feed upon the nutrients and acidify the milk, thereby encouraging the growth of beneficial microorganisms. These bacteria also make nutrients in the milk more bioavailable and lend pleasant odours and tastes.

It is said that there are more than four hundred different types of fermented milk products consumed around the world.[3] Almost every culture in Africa, the Middle East, Europe and India has an

Kazakh postage stamp in tribute to koumiss, a drink of fermented mare's milk. Believed to have medicinal properties, koumiss counted among its advocates such figures as writer Leo Tolstoy and composer Alexander Scriabin. It belongs to the category of a yeast-lactic ferment, which it shares with its cow's milk cousins, kefir and viili.

impressive variety of them. Most of them are mesophilic, fermenting at room temperature and lending themselves to backslopping, in which a small portion of an earlier batch serves as a starter for the next. It goes into making *filmjölk*, a tart, liquid milk product native to Sweden, and *matsoni*, a creamy yoghurt from Armenia. Simpler than backslopping is allowing bacteria already in the milk to ferment it. Yoghurt-like *ergo* is made this way in Ethiopia, as is *roub*, a similar product from the Sudan. Zimbabweans make *amasi* by storing unpasteurized milk in a hollowed calabash or hide sack and allowing it to ferment. And the peoples of the Himalayas collect the solids from freshly churned buttermilk for *churkam*, a naturally fermented cheese.

The origins of milk fermentation practices reach into the remote past. Scholars believe that dairying – production, storage and distribution of milk products – occurred some 15,000 years ago in the Middle East. Peoples of the region were then transitioning from a nomadic to a sedentary, agricultural mode of life. North African rock art of the fifth millennium BCE depicts cattle being herded by early Saharan pastoral groups, and pot shards from around the same period were discovered to have traces of milk fat still on them.[4] Sumerian seals dating somewhat later, 3200 BCE or so, depict young cattle or sheep in the act of exiting a hut while accompanied by female adults. Seals from later centuries depict men in the act of milking cows and processing what they gathered.[5]

East of Mesopotamia dairy products enjoyed no less importance. Hindu scriptures describe the birthplace of the sun, moon and stars as a vast sea of milk, an altogether fitting image for the limitless source of nutrition and life the stuff was believed to be. It appears that Indians of antiquity consumed mostly fermented milk products. They are mentioned in the Vedas, a collection of ancient religious literature. The Rigveda, whose date of 1700 BCE makes it the oldest work of the collection, contains over seven hundred references to cows and the plenty they represent. So healthful did

Vedic Indians find it that they used it as medicine as well as food. And so healthful did they find its source that they conferred on cows and other dairy animals special status. Cows earned the epithet *kamadugha*, or that which yields 'objects of desire like milk'.[6]

Though many would desire it, few would enjoy it. Many dairy delights became the exclusive fare of the elite Brahmin class, members of which often mixed milk or yoghurt with soma, a plant extract believed to confer immortality and enable communion with the gods.[7] As a beverage, milk was something of a luxury in the East and the West alike. Most people drank beer and wine. If they consumed any dairy at all they usually ate cheese, which stood with vegetable ferments as one of the few protein- and nutrient-rich foods they could get with any regularity. Transformation to cheese concentrated the nutrients in fluid milk and increased their bioavailability. It also preserved that nutrition in a form for easy transport and trade. Little wonder, then, that cheese became one of the most important fermented dairy products.

\* \* \*

Cheesemaking developed alongside other forms of dairying. The prevailing theory holds that its discovery came by way of observation that milk curdled in the sacks in which it was kept. This owed to the fact that the sacks were made of animal stomachs, and as such they contained residues of rennin, an enzyme that digests proteins. The resulting curds could be salted, pressed and dried into a palatable foodstuff that resembled cottage cheese or feta. Petrified balls of dried buttermilk unearthed by archaeologists had had holes bored through their centres, possibly so they could be strung together and hung for drying.[8]

No one can say where cheese first originated, only that its making was widespread. Pot shards discovered at a Neolithic site in Poland contained small holes. These suggest that the shards had once formed strainers for separating curds from whey.[9] The tombs

Hieroglyph depicting Egyptian cheesemaking. Cheese has its roots in remote antiquity, having been discovered to be coeval with the earliest civilizations.

of the Egyptian pharaoh Hor-Aha (*fl.* 3100 BCE) included among his wares for the afterlife two jars containing cheese – one cheese from Upper Egypt, another from Lower.[10] And included in the tomb of Ptahmes, a mayor of Egypt's one-time capital Memphis, was a pot of cheese dating to 1300 BCE. (Ptahmes's cheese also bore signs of the presence of *Brucella*, a bacterium that causes the high temperature, chills, sweats and weakness symptomatic of brucellosis, or 'Malta fever'.) In Sumer, cuneiform tablets from the Third Dynasty of Ur in the second millennium BCE record exchanges of cheese. And evidence of cheesemaking in 1615 BCE has been found in Xinjiang, China.[11]

Early literature makes frequent mention of cheese. 'Hath thou not poured me out as milk, and curdled me like cheese?', asks the biblical Job of the Lord. Aristotle likened the creation of a foetus to the making of cheese. Acting on a woman's menstrual blood, a man's semen causes the 'more solid part [of it to come] together', he wrote. Then, 'the liquid is separated off from it, and as the earthy parts solidify membranes form all round it'.[12] Homer's *Odyssey* features a dairy-loving cyclops, Polyphemus. 'Here crates were standing, loaded down with cheese,' remarks Odysseus upon entering the cyclops's cave. 'Swimming with whey were all the vessels, the well-wrought pails and bowls in which he milked.'[13]

In their detailed accounts of early cheesemaking the Romans were unsurpassed. The first-century CE writer Columella, who described so thoroughly the making of wine and other agricultural pursuits, saw it as an eminently practical matter for those who lived a great distance from town, deeming it better to make cheese than to carry 'the milk-pail to market'. For curdling the pail's contents he recommended lamb or kid's rennet. Wild thistle flowers, the seeds of 'bastard-saffron' (*Carthamus tinctorius*) and twigs or sap from a fig tree would also have done the job, this last alternative making for an exceedingly sweet cheese. Columella urged his readers to drain whey as quickly as possible, to press fresh curds into moulds or wicker baskets, and to weigh the moulds or baskets down. After a rest of nine days the cheese could be put away in 'a dark and cold place' for ripening. He further recommended that makers brine their cheese for a few days and dry it in the sun before eating it.[14]

From the few steps elaborated by Columella came dozens of kinds of Roman cheese. Pliny the Elder wrote that the best kind arrived from the province of Nemausus (present-day Nîmes, France, and environs) – the villages of Lesura and Gabalis, particularly. Because it was quite perishable, however, it had to have been eaten fresh. Pliny also praised Docleatian and Vatusican cheeses, both from the Alps, and a certain smoked goat's cheese from Rome. (A cheese from Gaul, however, put him off with its strongly medicinal flavour.) He claimed that a soak in thyme-infused vinegar would revive cheese whose zest had left it. The trick had noble – indeed, holy – precedent and reportedly worked to

A modern recreation of the spreadable herbed-cheese dish moretum, which was popular in ancient Rome. As they had for wine, Romans advanced and refined the art of cheesemaking, creating various offerings from the milk of goats, sheep, cows and even rabbits.

astonishing effect. 'It is said that Zoroaster lived thirty years in the wilderness upon cheese prepared in such a peculiar manner', Pliny wrote, 'that he was insensible to the advances of old age.'[15]

Romans of all classes ate cheese. Farmers and other rustic types, to whom pungency and strong garlic flavour presented no difficulty, ate a herbed cheese spread called *moretum*. Recipes for sweeter fare were recorded by Roman senator and historian Cato the Elder, who in *De agricultura* includes a recipe for *placenta*, a rich cheesecake that consists of layers of dough and honeyed sheep's cheese. Also presented is a recipe for a simpler cheesecake, *libum*, in which cheese, cornmeal and eggs are brayed in a mortar and baked slowly under a dish and over a hot hearthstone. But woe unto the one who overindulged in such delights. Romans thought cheese could weigh heavily upon the stomach and cause gas and other digestive upsets. For those whose bowels rumbled, Pliny the Elder suggested cheese made from rabbit's milk as a more agreeable substitute.

Ancient Romans had no taste for fresh milk; unless directed otherwise for medical reasons, members of the wealthy and middle classes avoided it altogether. This aversion the Romans inherited from the Greeks, who thought that fresh milk caused everything from obesity to sterility and laziness. Only barbarians would risk these afflictions. The fifth-century BCE Greek historian Herodotus noted the Scythians' fondness for mare's milk and their strange way of getting it. Enlisting the aid of blind slaves, they would thrust 'tubes made of bone, not unlike our musical pipes, up the vulva of the mare', Herodotus writes. Following the insertion, the Scythians or their slaves would blow 'into the tubes with their mouths, some milking while others blow'. This unique method supposedly filled the animal's veins with air, which in turn caused its udder to drop.[16] Some three centuries later, Julius Caesar would describe the British tribes as living on 'milk and flesh', a diet that likely struck the Roman conqueror as lacking in refinement.

The milk drinkers would nonetheless prevail over their Roman occupiers. After the fall of the Empire, peasants and Christian monks continued to make cheese, or 'white meat' as it came to be called, and it proved an important source of protein. Yet unlike the sweated peasantry, who needed rough-and-ready sustenance, monks enjoyed leisure and stability enough for the more deliberate crafting of cheese. They experimented culinarily and produced a variety of delicious results.

Sometimes this prowess in cheesemaking became a liability. While travelling between Paris and Aachen, his royal residence in present-day western Germany, Emperor Charlemagne stopped at a bishop's estate for dinner. His visit occurred on a holy day, which meant he could eat neither meat nor poultry. The bishop had happened to run out of fish, an acceptable substitute. He did

Illuminated manuscript detail depicting cheesemaking in the Middle Ages. The cheese consumed by peasants tended to be rustic and simple yet nourishing. Production of finer cheeses meanwhile fell to monks, who had the time for the additional trouble to which the task put them.

have cheese on hand, however – a kind that today is Brie. This he served to his esteemed guest, who proceeded to eat its creamy inside, pushing aside the white rind. Observing this, the bishop told Charlemagne that he had refused 'the best part'. Charlemagne took his host at his word, ate the rind and pronounced it delicious, 'like butter'. In fact, so taken with the cheese was he that he promptly ordered the bishop to send him every year two cartloads of it to his court at Aachen.[17]

\*\*\*

The bishop's estate was likely already somewhere near the emperor's court, for soft cheeses did not travel well. Nor were they meant to.

The fact that many monasteries made soft, 'bloomy-rind' cheeses suggests a priority for satisfying local demand. A cheese's market – how near or not it was to the site of production, specifically – determined its characteristics. Soft cheeses were made close to the cities in which they were sold. Hard cheeses stood up to transit over rough roads and heavy seas. For this reason the site of their production need not have lain terribly close to their markets. Also for this reason they became lucrative exports. The countries that excelled in making them grew rich.

In this respect, Parmesan cheese is exemplary. Developed in northern Italy sometime in the fourteenth century, it became the darling of Tuscan merchants, who sold it everywhere from northern Africa to the coastal towns of France and Spain, its high salt content and low moisture enabling it to keep its zest in hot climes. It became a favourite wherever it was sold. The British diarist Samuel Pepys so loved Parmesan cheese that he buried some along with other of his belongings he hoped to spare from the Great Fire of London in 1666.

In time, other high-salt, low-moisture cheeses came to join Parmesan on the global market. Out in front of this development were, once again, the Dutch, whose genius for business helped them to excel in the trade. Cheese and beer were the pillars of the Dutch economy, and they were all many Dutch people consumed. In an account of his visit to the Netherlands, an English statesman relates how the country's citizens 'were us'd to be call'd Blockheads, and eaters of Cheese and Milk'. Printed matter in the British Isles followed suit. One pamphlet described a Dutchman as 'a lusty, Fat, Two-Legged Cheese-Worm'.[18] Yet for all the disparagement they endured, the lusty blockheads became one of the most prosperous and well-fed peoples in Europe, thanks in large part to cheese.

As it did with the beer trade, the Dutch government positioned farmers and tradesmen for great success in the cheese trade. They transformed land that consisted largely of peat bogs and salt pastures into fields amenable to dairying. They drained lakes, built dykes and windmills, and grew fodder for dairy cows on available parcels of land. The last they enriched with their own night soil – manure from collected human excrement – along with cow dung and ash from soap boilers. The Dutch selected milch cows of great size and yields, each said to have given about 1,350 litres (357 U.S. gallons) of milk per year.[19] (Modern Holsteins give about 908 litres (240 U.S. gallons) per *month*.)

Thus transformed, the Netherlands' rural hinterlands fed its growing cities like never before. Milk came to form the backbone of the national diet – and a much celebrated one at that. The seventeenth-century humanist Heijman Jacobi wrote that a diet of 'sweet milk, fresh bread, good mutton and beef, fresh butter and cheese' brought one sound health. Three members of that sextet came from the robust dairy industry alone, such was the abundance and affordability of the stuff. It seemed that everyone, no matter how rich or poor, ate them. A man of humble means could butter his bread before covering it with cheese or meat. (The English considered this an example of the Dutch people's unbecoming extravagance.) Even orphans and vagrants sipped milk and supped on cheese. For the working classes, dairy products served as a protein-rich fuel to power them through their toil; for the middle class, they served, in their seemingly endless variety, as an ever-novel delight to fetch them from boredom. In his *Travels Through the Low-Countries: Germany, Italy, and France*, seventeenth-century British naturalist John Ray wrote of 'four or five sorts of cheese' that 'they usually bring forth and set before you'.[20]

What Ray observed was not uncommon. For every occasion and appetite there was a cheese to suit it, and each cheese had a unique savour. Cheeses for the parlour and its comforts were small, round and deliciously fresh, for instance, and cheeses for sea voyages were covered with turmeric, saffron and other preservative herbs that added a piquancy likely savoured by famished sailors.

Illustration by Rachael Robinson Elmer for 'The Boy Who Wanted More Cheese', in *Dutch Fairy Tales for Young Folks* by William Elliot Griffis (1918). Thanks to a policy initiative by the Dutch government, cheesemaking in the Netherlands boomed, and cheese became one of the country's most abundant foodstuffs – so abundant as perhaps to seem borne to shop shelves and pantries by fairies.

Such a diversity of cheese offerings rewarded the Dutch handsomely. The 1640s saw the city of Gouda selling nearly 2.3 million kg (5 million lb) of cheese per year. By the 1670s, the figure exceeded 2.7 million kg (6 million lb).[21] Joining Gouda as cheese-exporting powerhouses were the cities of Alkmaar, Rotterdam, Amsterdam and Hoorn, the last of which boasting as its market the whole of Europe.[22]

The Netherlands' cheese supremacy appears all the more remarkable in light of the fact that knowledge of microbes and their actions was incomplete through most of the seventeenth century. Not until 1665 would Robert Hooke observe 'Blue and White and several kinds of hairy mouldy spots' on cheese, and the world would have to wait another two hundred years before anyone would do anything with this observation.[23] Before that moment arrived, cheese continued to be made, as it had for thousands of years, through the time-honoured approach of trial and error.

Yet it also involved deeply interwoven influences of individuals, animals and local conditions. Technique and terroir combined to determine the taste and texture of a cheese. Animals that grazed on clover growing in mineral-rich soil produced a different kind of milk than animals that nibbled on mountain herbs. A cheese's microbes could come from any source – milking utensils, the wind, even a dairy maid herself. To this invisible confusion a cheese variety owed its signature flavours. A food intimately tied to its locality, cheese had long resisted trammelling into reliably standard and homogeneous kinds for export to market.

Despite subsequent innovations that led to commercial viability on a global scale, the fundamentals of cheesemaking remained unchanged. (Indeed, they are practised on many farmsteads today.) Milk was heated, inoculated with a starter culture and curdled with rennet or some other coagulant. The degree of coagulation determined the cheese's final moisture content and its speed of fermentation. For example, the curds for Brillat-Savarin – a soft cheese named in honour of the French author of *The Physiology of Taste*, a pioneering work of food writing published in 1825 – were gently separated from the whey in order to preserve most of the moisture; whereas the curds of the hard cheese Emmentaler were cut by large steel combs, a technique that expelled more whey. The finer the curd was cut, the harder the cheese became. Once cut, the curds were drained, piled into moulds or hoops and pressed. They were then turned out of the moulds, rubbed with salt and soaked in brine.

The exact process depended, of course, on the variety of the cheese. Sometimes the curds were heated. Cheeses set aside for ageing were placed in a cold cellar or cave to ripen. Often their rinds were washed beforehand with brine to harden them for travel and long storage. Brie and other 'bloomy-rind' cheeses, which were not intended to travel far, were aged a few weeks and then placed in wooden boxes to protect their delicate rind. And all the while the microbes worked their magic, transforming a mass of curds into a delicately flavoured mascarpone, an earthy Stinking Bishop or one of the other hundreds of varieties of cheese. For the ripening, microclimate determined all. The flavour of a single kind of cheese could vary depending on the season in which a particular wheel was made or the day on which it was eaten.[24]

\* \* \*

The formerly ineluctable chance elements of cheesemaking would cede to standardization in the nineteenth century. Burgeoning industry realized the possibility of mass production of cheese. Keen incentive to do so existed. Cheese recommended itself as the perfect food for factory workers. It resisted spoilage, contained rich amounts of protein and vital nutrients, and was toothsome and satisfying if made properly. In 1851 the father–son duo of Jesse and George Williams of Rome, New York, built dedicated facilities for making and ageing cheese. The facilities, which they kept separate from their farms nearby, could handle large quantities of milk. In its first season of operation, the Williamses' factory produced 45,360 kg (100,000 lb) of stirred-curd cheese, a yield five times that of a good-sized farmstead operation.[25]

The venture proved a tremendous success. The Williamses found that they could produce massive amounts of cheese and save on labour and supply costs into the bargain. What is more, their cheese achieved a reliable and therefore predictable consistency that resisted the vicissitudes of terroir and season. Plus, it was cheaper to make and therefore cheaper to sell, a merit that helped their Cheddar to dominate the cheese market.

Improvements to the Williamses' industrial method came in 1866. That year the American Dairymen's Association introduced cheese manufacturers to a more scientific approach to cheesemaking, one that had exact specifications for temperature and acidity, as well as exact times for fermentation.

The approach spurred the growth of Cheddar cheese factories throughout the state of New York, for the combined forces of industrialization and war had spurred demand. Millions of women, their domestic burdens having increased with their husbands fighting in the American Civil War, chose to buy factory-made cheese rather than make their own at home.[26] Demand also grew across the Atlantic as the British imported cheese to feed a burgeoning factory workforce. For not only was factory cheese convenient, it was cheap. The shortened fermentation time left more water in the cheese. Since the cheese was sold by weight, water served to

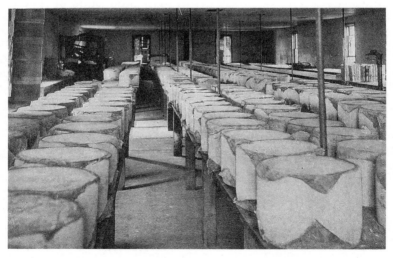

Rows of cheese curing in an industrial facility. In the 19th century cheesemaking became big business as understanding of the process became more scientific and exact, which led to standardization and a subsequent leap in productive output.

reduce the price. And though it also happened to kill the cheese's zest, demand soared nonetheless.[27]

Soaring demand unfortunately prompted manufacturers to employ dishonest practices such as using fillers, skimming cream and replacing cream with lard. However, adulteration eventually brought about the slide of the United States as the dominant Cheddar cheese-producing nation, as importers turned to Canada and Australia for a better product.[28]

Meanwhile, scientific progress in manufacturing proceeded apace. In the early years of the twentieth century Charles Thom, a mycologist from the Storrs Agricultural Experiment Station in Connecticut, adapted European farmstead practices to industrial cheesemaking, identifying the moulds essential to producing cheeses such as Roquefort and Brie. A dedicated farmer brusque in manner, Thom believed science could unlock the secrets to artisanal cheesemaking. In 1899, he earned the first doctorate ever awarded by the University of Missouri. Four years later he headed cheese investigations at the Storrs station. In his *The Book of Cheese*, published in 1918, Thom wrote that the art of cheesemaking 'has been developed to high stages of perfection in widely separate localities', and that '[t]he practices of making and handling such cheese have been developed in intimate relation to climate, local conditions and the habits of the people.' So important is this relationship between food and place that 'the removal of expert makers of such cheeses to new regions has resulted in total failure to transplant the industry.' Yet a scientific understanding of the 'the nature of the micro-organisms in milk, and the methods of controlling them' could stand in for this expert knowledge.[29]

This conviction marked the beginning of a long and fruitful career with the United States Department of Agriculture. There Thom brought traditional European cheesemaking to the modern American factory by replicating the conditions under which the desired microflora could flourish. He found particular success

Cheesemaking facility worker packing a wrapped wheel of Roquefort for shipment. The sanitation craze of the early 20th century tipped the market in favour of industrial cheesemakers, whose ability to pasteurize, process and seal their product appealed to microbe-fearing consumers willing to sacrifice flavour for peace of mind.

with the moulds *Penicillium camemberti* and *Penicillium roqueforti*. *Penicillium* and *Aspergillus* later became objects of enquiry, and he became a world authority on them. Thom would go on to develop and refine numerous other fermentative processes.[30] Thanks to him, millions of Americans could enjoy European cheeses.

Commercial cheesemaking advanced yet again in the 1930s, thanks to single-strain starter cultures, which supplanted earlier methods of backslopping and wild inoculation.[31] Meanwhile, economic depression and, later, the economic pressures of industrial farming liquidated many farmsteads and, with them, their cheeses.

With the liquidation of farmstead cheeses came a thoroughgoing mechanization of cheesemaking. The sanitation and asepsis associated with such a process bred in consumers a wholly new attitude towards the final product. 'Americans "kill" their cheese through pasteurization,' writes contemporary French cultural anthropologist and marketing expert Clotaire Rapaille; they 'select hunks of cheese that have been prewrapped – mummified, if you will – in plastic (like body bags), and store it, still wrapped airtight, in a morgue also known as a refrigerator'.[32] (Rapaille and his countrymen and -women prefer to keep their cheese at room temperature by storing it under a cloche.) For Rapaille, the word most closely associated with processed cheese is 'death'. And dead indeed were the legions of microorganisms that for millennia had added zest and complexity to an otherwise all-too-familiar food for people of few means.

\* \* \*

Thanks to the work of a melancholy zoologist and eventual Nobel Prize laureate, other kinds of fermented dairy would continue to mean life.

In 1888 Pasteur invited the zoologist in question, Élie Metchnikoff, to study at his eponymous institute in Paris. Born in 1845 in a small Ukrainian village, Metchnikoff would go on to become the father of immunology, winning the Nobel Prize in 1908 for his discovery of macrophages – the white blood cells found at infection sites – which he happened upon while inserting thorns into starfish. From this and other findings he developed elaborate theories about the relationship between bacteria and ageing.

Metchnikoff was in the middle of these investigations into immune response when he took up Pasteur's offer. At the Institute he continued his work. His time there, however, was marred by chronic indigestion. He drank sour milk daily in a bid to remedy it. One day a colleague introduced him to Bulgarian yoghurt. The unusual food intrigued him, as did its apparent effects: the peasants who ate it often lived to an unusually advanced age. Metchnikoff surmised that their longevity somehow owed to their yoghurt consumption. In 1908 he shared his theory during a public lecture on old age. He adjured the audience to avoid raw food, which he believed to be covered in germs, and moreover to consume yoghurt for the effects it had on harmful intestinal bacteria. His words were taken to heart: his lecture sparked a vogue for sour milk, and people used it to cure everything from diarrhoea in infants to sluggish bowels in adults.[33]

Metchnikoff further publicized his ideas in his work *The Prolongation of Life: Optimistic Studies*, whose English translation appeared in 1907. Therein he dilated on his idea that, though most bacteria do produce toxins that cause illness, there did exist a class of microbes that could extend life. Like Pasteur, Metchnikoff noted that lactic acid bacteria could transform food. He presented examples: sour milk can become 'many kinds of cheese' and vegetables undergo a 'natural process of souring', such as happens in sauerkraut, rye bread, kvass and sour milk.[34]

He was not the first to note this. In 1780 Swedish chemist Carl Wilhelm Scheele identified lactic acid bacteria in sour milk. (An apparent expert in all things invisible, Scheele is also credited with discovering oxygen in 1773.[35]) Yet his discovery was forgotten only to be rediscovered in 1813, when Henri Braconnot, director of the Botanical Garden of Nancy, observed bacteria once again living on fermented rice, spoiled beet juice and moistened baker's yeast. The by-product of the bacterial activity he dubbed acid of Nancy.[36] It was not until Pasteur looked at lactic acid yeast and butyric acid from spoiled butter that lactic acid bacteria came under any systematic study. In 1873 the British surgeon Joseph Lister discovered that *Streptococcus* bacteria caused milk to clot. From the clotted milk he isolated a pure culture that he called *Bacterium lactis*.[37]

Metchnikoff's research suggested such transformations were especially healthful. The ability of lactic acid to halt putrefaction prompted Metchnikoff to ask, 'As lactic fermentation serves so well to arrest putrefaction in general, why should it not be used for the same purpose within the digestive tube?'[38]

Metchnikoff set about showing that lactic fermentation not only should, it could. He scoured the literature for examples of centenarian drinkers of sour milk. He learned of one labourer in Verdun who 'ate nothing but unleavened bread and drank nothing but skimmed milk' for all of his III years before passing in 1751; of one Marie Priou of Haute-Garonne who died in 1838 reportedly at the age of 158 years, her diet in the final decade of her life nothing but cheese and goat's milk; and of a 180-year-old (!) woman in the Caucasus, still living as of Metchnikoff's survey, who did her own housework, abstained from liquor and subsisted on barley bread and buttermilk taken after churning cream. 'Butter milk is a liquid containing very many lactic microbes,' Metchnikoff

Élie Metchnikoff in his laboratory. Prompted by the uncommon longevity and health of rural Bulgarians, who depended on sour dairy as a staple food, the Ukrainian-born zoologist began experiments that led to his discovery of beneficial lactic acid bacteria.

reminds readers, lest they should doubt his examples.[39] 'From time immemorial human beings have absorbed quantities of lactic microbes by consuming in the uncooked condition substances such as soured milk, kephir, sauerkraut, or salted cucumbers which have undergone lactic fermentation,' he continues. 'By these means they have unknowingly lessened the evil consequences of intestinal putrefaction.'[40]

Some suspect examples notwithstanding, Metchnikoff's general claim as to fermented dairy's healthfulness found purchase. Industrial yoghurt-making kicked off in Barcelona, Spain, in 1919. By 1925 the fermented foodstuff's growing popularity had begun to register in literature. One character in the English writer Evelyn Waugh's *A Handful of Dust* dutifully spoons up 'her morning yoghourt' every day.[41] The 1970s saw Metchnikoff's theories given renewed attention by advertising. Executives with the Marstellar agency came across research by American physician and scientist Alexander Leaf, who claimed that a diet high in yoghurt explained the longevity enjoyed by the people of Georgia, then a part of the Union of Soviet Socialist Republics. The agency's discovery could not have been more felicitous; it showed the way to campaign on behalf of their client Dannon – Danone outside the u.s. – a company whose signature product, yoghurt, had hit a sales slump. Through diplomats the agency secured permission to film television commercials from the Soviet government, which declared itself eager to cooperate. The advert was filmed in 1976 and aired as part of a campaign a year later. 'In Soviet Georgia there are two curious things about the people', declares a voiceover in one advert: 'a large part of their diet is yogurt, and a large number of them live past 100.' Shots of Georgians hoeing, tending plants, riding horseback and, of course, eating Dannon yoghurt play under the narration, each subject hale and upright despite his advanced age.[42]

A print advertisement that ran as part of the campaign delivered the message in a pithier way. Its single image was that of an

Photo taken of one Mme Robineau, reportedly on the occasion of her 105th birthday. The French centenarian was one of several studied by Élie Metchnikoff in his attempt to fathom the mystery of longevity and fermented dairy's role in it.

elderly woman in traditional garb at a table. The tip of the spoon in her hand hovers near the rim of a Dannon yoghurt container. Bowls of fruit and other wholesome foods occupy the foreground. Below the image a caption reads: 'One of Soviet Georgia's senior citizens thought Dannon was an excellent yogurt. She ought to know. She's been eating yogurt for 137 years.' The first advertisements to feature stills and footage captured behind the Iron Curtain, Marstellar's campaign on behalf of Dannon also won kudos for its quality.[43]

It emerged after the campaign that the featured Georgians were neither as old as they claimed (birth records of Georgian towns and villages were spotty at best) nor avid yoghurt eaters. Yet by that time the message had made its impact, starting a vogue that survived into the present.

Yoghurt is once again a beloved food of the health- and mortality-conscious, who today enjoy the added boon of a wider selection of variants to choose from. Jostling with yoghurt on store shelves these days are such offerings as kefir, skyr (an Icelandic cultured dairy product similar in consistency to Greek yoghurt yet milder in flavour) and quark, a mild dairy product of European origin.

The variety translates into healthy profits. Kefir alone will see sales of over $2 billion by 2025, industry soothsayers predict.[44] And though a diet rich in dairy ferments may not guarantee you a one-hundredth birthday party, it will deliver benefits in the here and now. As we will see in the final chapter, more robust immunity and greater general well-being are but two of the upsides of a diet rich in curdled cow's milk.

# 7 Tasty but Dangerous: The Virtues and Risks of Sausage and Fermented Meats

When the girl came into the kitchen in the morning at
the busiest moment of the day's work, they grasped hands
over the dishes of sausage-meat. Sometimes she helped him,
holding the skins with her plump fingers while he filled them
with meat and fat. Sometimes, too, with the tips of their
tongues they just tasted the raw sausage-meat, to see if it
was properly seasoned.
– Émile Zola, *The Fat and the Thin* (1873)[1]

CALLED 'WHITE MEAT' BY the poor who subsisted on it, cheese
provided the protein essential for balancing an otherwise largely
farinaceous diet. Any real meat the poor ate likely came in the form
of sausage, ham and other fermented, salted, cured or otherwise
processed products. Like cheese, many of these processed meats
were preserved with lactic acid bacteria. Yet unlike cheese, whose
uniformly light coloration limited the adulterants that could be
added to it, such fermented meats as sausage and ham could
contain any number of noxious and dangerous ingredients. 'In
meat,' once admitted an agent of the United States Department
of Agriculture to food writer Waverley Root, 'we've got a product

not only subject to easy contamination but extremely amenable to adulteration and to concealment of adulteration.'²

Any such easy contamination and amenability to adulteration held just as true in earlier centuries, well before the coinage of the now familiar saying about the ill-advised wish for seeing 'how the sausage is made'. Throughout history, fermented meat was a food eaten in a spirit of trust or desperation, if not an uneasy mixture of both.

Before humanity practised sedentary agriculture it preserved meat, which was as perishable as it was abundant. (It has emerged recently that as much as 400,000 years ago humans stashed bones as a way of preserving the marrow within.³) Inhabitants of dry, temperate regions had an advantage when it came to this task. The challenge lay in removing moisture from, say, a haunch of deer or buffalo. Drying presented a quick way of doing this, and smoke lent additional antimicrobial effects. These techniques remained crude and uncertain, however; a portion of meat submitted to them may have spoilt just as well as kept.

Preservation techniques improved with time. Meat was costly, a relative luxury as food goes. Its purveyors had tremendous incentive for finding use for every scrap. Though scholars remain uncertain as to the first historical appearance of sausage, there is evidence that Mesopotamians filled intestinal casings with forcemeat some 4,000 years ago, and that as early as 2,500 years ago, Babylonians were fermenting their encased forcemeat. Yet the art of sausage-making would see its greatest refinements in the ancient Mediterranean.⁴ The Greeks developed an impressive variety of sausages, many of them pork-based and richly seasoned with herbs and spices. In the *Odyssey*, Homer at one point likens Odysseus, newly arrived to Ithaca and consumed with dispatching Penelope's suitors, to a sausage made of 'fat and blood' turned 'to and fro' over a fire as a way of illustrating his titular hero's agitation.⁵

Meat drying outdoors in Maranhão, Brazil. The practice of drying meat reaches into human prehistory. It represented the best way for peoples on the move to preserve a food that spoiled easily and required much effort to secure.

Though early sausages contained all kinds of fillings and seasonings, they were all made by backslopping; that is, inoculation with the bacteria that would ferment them. Sausage-makers set aside some 5 to 25 per cent of their forcemeat, depending on the recipe, for use in future batches. Inoculum in such large amounts forfended against invasion and takeover of the mixture by harmful microbes – a fairly reliable method for small batches. Multiple strains lived in an inoculum. If a strain died, a stronger one simply replaced it.

Making their home in sausage forcemeat were mostly homofermentative lactic acid bacteria, of which many are related to *Lactobacillus plantarum*. Also present may have been beneficial *Lactobacillus casei* and *Lactobacillus leichmannii* bacteria, harmless yeasts and moulds, and harmful enterococci and *Listeria*. The exact mix of microorganisms depended on a subtle play of factors, including ingredients, atmosphere, temperature, air circulation and presence of salt and other additives.[6] Salami and similar naturally

Carle Vernet, *The Sausage Seller*, 1861, etching. Perhaps the most common and familiar of fermented meats, sausage owes its great variety as much to the specific homofermentative lactic acid bacteria that comes to colonize its forcemeat and the mycoflora that colonize its casing as it does to the blend of ingredients with which it is prepared.

dried sausage would begin their ripening with some 95 per cent of their mycoflora on their surface. As the sausage's moisture decreased over two weeks, the amounts of moulds and yeast would become equal. At the ripening's end, moulds remained as the dominant microorganism.[7] All the while, lactic acid bacteria set to work on the forcemeat, lowering its pH and making it inhospitable to other microorganisms. The resulting product, should nothing go awry, was sausage much like the kind eaten today.[8]

The road from early sausage to modern ran through Rome. As they had with wine and cheese, ancient Romans pioneered techniques of sausage-making. Their invention likely rested on necessity: their sacrifices and other religious rites left them with ample supplies of blood for filling – though a suspicion did prevail that the filling came from the flesh of plague-stricken mules and stolen meat smuggled between the sausage-maker's buttocks. Usually, the forcemeat consisted of meat, blood, fat and offal, which Roman sausage-makers stuffed into intestines and stomachs by means of a cloth funnel. Thus prepared, the sausage then fermented in caves rich in beneficial microorganisms and was later smoked over fires of birch and oak.[9]

Roman sausage came in two shapes: fat and bag-like, and long and narrow. The first-century CE gourmand Apicius recorded recipes for both. One calls for hard-boiled eggs, pine kernels, onions, leeks and much blood. This sausage was known as *botellum*. The narrower variety of sausage, called *lucanian*, was perhaps the most popular among Romans. To make it, Apicius writes, pepper, cumin, savoury, rue, parsley, mixed herbs, laurel berries and liquamen, a fermented fish sauce, are pounded together, mixed with fat and meat (mostly pork), forced into skins, drawn out until sufficiently narrow, and finally smoked. Lucanian sausage is believed to be the ancestor of numerous northern Italian sausages, many of which are made in a similar fashion today.[10]

Sausages of the kinds described by Apicius were eaten throughout the empire. Long sausages aged in the rafters of inns and taverns until they were ready to be sold to hungry patrons. Sausage sellers stalked urban thoroughfares. The poet Martial complained about the noise caused by the 'pie man who bawls as he carries round his warm pans of smoking sausages'.[11] Petronius' *Satyricon* features an elaborate feast hosted by the wealthy freedman Trimalchio. The sumptuous dishes on offer include a roast pig whose stuffing of pudding and sausage was likely made from the creature's own blood and entrails. In Ovid's tale of Philemon and Baucis, smoked hams hang in the humble kitchen in which the titular householders receive their divine guests.

Yet sausage managed to rise above the quotidian, gaining an association with the divine and playing an important role in pagan rites. In the Lupercalia, a festival dedicated to the goat god Pan held during the emperor Nero's reign (54–68 CE), naked youths danced in the streets and brandished whips for lashing women, who begged for such treatment in the belief that it helped to keep them youthful, as platters of sausages were served forth. So important were sausages to this most riotous of festivals that Emperor Constantine banned both when he converted to Christianity. The food's suggestive shape disgusted Christians, who also blanched at the blood that was frequently an ingredient. The censure of an ascendant Christendom did little to diminish sausages' appeal. The phallic food went underground, where it thrived on the black market through the Dark Ages.[12]

Though sausage found a home in markets, black or otherwise, from the time of its invention, it did not find a home in every

Andrea Cammassei, *Lupercalia*, c. 1635, oil on canvas. Sausage was the featured food item at this raucous festival in which Roman women sought eternal youth and beauty. The period of the late Empire was to be the final heyday for sausage in antiquity. It would have to await the Middle Ages before it would again be considered a respectable dish.

climate. Conditions of low humidity and ample sunshine were required for making it well. The northernmost parts of Europe presented special difficulties. Cultures of those regions therefore turned to alternatives. Norwegians had their *fenalår*. To make it, they hung a salted sheep's leg in a climate-controlled area, where a tenderizing mould colonized it. They then smoked it, which kept spoilage organisms from forming in wet weather, and dried it in traditional storage houses set on pillars. Nomadic shepherds of western Norway 3,000 years ago ate *fenalår*, as did the Vikings, for whom it had the added virtue of withstanding the rigours of seafaring. Dark red in colour and tasting distinctly of the animal from which it was made, it was usually served with unfermented crispbread, eggs and beer.[13] For millennia *fenalår* played an important role in the northern European diet, where the rocky soil and short days made farming difficult.

The harsh conditions of northern Europe extended to its island nations. In Iceland, where, like Norway, keeping sheep was common, the inhabitants pickled sheep meat in whey, or they dried and smoked it. One such dried and smoked meat was *hangikjöt*, a traditional holiday dish. To make it, Icelanders butchered a freshly killed sheep into legs, forequarters, rack and flanks. The meat of each they soaked in water, salted and smoked for two or three weeks over an open fire, usually in the kitchen. The fire may have burned peat, sheep dung and birch wood, each kind of fuel imparting unique flavours. Newly smoked meat then went into a hut for drying and storage ahead of any coming festive event.[14]

The harsher the climate, the more important a food did fermented meat become. The Saami of northernmost Finland fermented reindeer meat, a dietary staple, with sea salt and lactic acid bacteria before rinsing and cold-smoking it over slow-burning alder, birch or juniper chips. The staples of Greenland reflected the indigenous Inuit hunting culture. Meat of whales, seals, walruses, caribou and other creatures dried on wooden poles high above the

Seal meat drying according to the traditional method. Along with the meats of other animals common in the Arctic region – caribou, whale, walrus – seal meat ferments with whatever ambient microorganisms manage to colonize it.

ground for several weeks before going into storage. It fermented entirely naturally; not even salt was used. Inuit would sometimes place meat and fat from these same animals in closed-skin bags, which they then buried on a gravel beach. There the bags' contents fermented for several weeks or months.[15] The people of Alaska made a similar food, aptly called 'stinkheads', by burying king salmon heads in the ground to spend months fermenting. Once ready, the heads were mashed into a mush for eating.

Stinkheads are just one example of fermented fish, a food popular the world over. Plentiful but perishable, fish had, until recently, been the food of the poor, and preserving the catch was of paramount importance. Fermented fish provided much-needed nutrients and protein in a diet that was usually lacking in both.

The fermentation process converts proteins, fat and glucose into peptides and amino acids, fatty acids and lactic acids through the action of enzymes and microorganisms.[16]

The high salt content favours bacteria tolerant of such a medium. The exact variety of bacteria changes as fermentation progresses. After about twenty days, predominant species are of *Lactobacillus*, as well as *Streptococcus* and *Pediococcus*.[17] Properly done, the process produces, depending on the moisture content, a highly nutritious paste or a liquid with a rich umami, owing to a high glutamate content.

Every part of the world had, and still has, its own twist on fermented fish. The Sudanese build temporary sheds in which to make *fessiekh*. Within those sheds they wash whole fresh fish, which they cover in salt and arrange in layers on mats, in baskets or in perforated drums to ferment for three to seven days, depending on climatic conditions. Once sufficiently fermented, they drain the fish before placing it in larger fermentation vessels and adding more salt. They cover the vessels and weigh the covers down, and their contents are left to ferment for another ten to fifteen days. Once ready, the fessiekh – which during fermentation achieves a soft texture, silvery sheen and pungent aroma – is canned or bagged for sale.[18]

Perhaps unsurprisingly, fermented fish abounds in the South Pacific. Indonesians make *bakasang* by mixing small fish or skipjack tuna guts with copious amounts of salt, drying the mixture in the sun for ten to fifteen days and fermenting it for about thirty days. A similar food, *patis*, is made in the Philippines and aged up to two years. And in Cambodia there is *prahok*, a paste made from cleaned, scaled and gutted mudfish or moonlight gourami (the latter is more closely associated with Laotian cuisine). Its makers crush the fish underfoot, sun-dry it and ferment it in large clay jars covered with woven bamboo lids. Although prahok is ready to eat after fermenting for three weeks, it tastes best after three years. Its

Prahok accompanied by rice and garnish. Also known as 'Cambodian cheese', this fermented fish dish boasts a most unappetizing method of preparation. Left to age anywhere from three weeks to three years, however, it acquires a signature bouquet and savour that have made it a traditional favourite.

piquant odour earned it the moniker 'Cambodian cheese', and it often accompanies beef or is served at the table as a dip.

\*\*\*

No matter the kind of animal flesh fermented, over the end product loomed the spectre of toxicity. More so than the microbes in bread, beer, wine or cheese, those in putrid meat products could kill. Added risk came from the pungent nature of meat ferments, which often made it difficult to tell whether a sausage or a fish paste had putrefied or merely fermented too long. (Whereas fermentation oxidizes carbohydrates, putrefaction largely degrades a meat's protein materials; it is also the term used to describe that which happens when undesirable bacteria take over a ferment.) In the tenth century, Byzantine emperor Leo vi banned blood sausages following an outbreak of food poisoning. Such outbreaks happened often, each time producing similar symptoms: impaired breathing, difficulty speaking, blurred vision. Though fermented meat aroused suspicion as a possible cause, no one knew how it managed to sicken people. At any rate, laws enacted to prevent or curb outbreaks met with only limited success.

A breakthrough would come in the nineteenth century. German medical officer Justinus Kerner betook himself to fathoming the connection between possibly putrid meat and poisoning. In 1820 he turned his attention to an outbreak that occurred in Württemberg some 27 years earlier. Seventy-six people fell ill and another 37 died from eating a certain type of sausage. Thick and heavy, it had stomach rather than intestine as a casing. Kerner also discovered that the forcemeat that went into such a large casing remained too moist for it to smoke properly in home chimneys, as had been the tradition. Kerner extracted from a sample of this sausage variety the substance he believed to have caused the illness. His first comprehensive description of sausage poisoning appeared in 1822. And with the courage peculiar to experimentalists of his time, Kerner sought to confirm his conclusions by injecting himself with the substance. It indeed made him ill. Fortunately, he survived.

As it turned out, Kerner had isolated the cause of botulism.[19] The offending microbe, *Clostridium botulinum*, flourished in fermenting animal flesh, finding it a hospitably warm, low-acidity environment. Kerner's findings thus prompted changes in the making of Württemberg's cherished sausage. Yet any such triumph in public health prevailed against immense pressure to produce fermented meats on a mass scale. The trouble was that sausage neither lent itself to mass production nor travelled well. A good percentage of the considerable number of sausages Germany exported to Britain in the 1880s, for instance, had turned putrid in transit. One prominent British physician recorded a case of a 42-year-old gardener who had eaten canned German sausage and

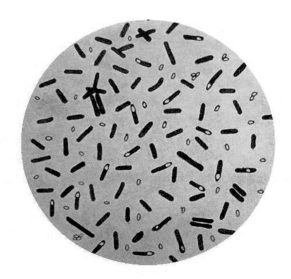

Colony of *Clostridium botulinum*. The deadly microorganism remained a hidden danger of canned meat well into the 20th century. It presented a particular problem for anyone eating fermented food from tins. She could never be completely certain whether she was tasting the effects of beneficial (fermentation) or harmful (putrefaction) bacteria.

suddenly fallen ill, the victim experiencing nausea, flushing, chills and laboured breathing. He lingered in this condition for eight days before dying.[20]

The gardener represented just one of a number of cases that investigators later traced to a kind of sausage immersed in melted fat and housed in a 'cylinder of tinned iron'.[21] Yet sausage kept equally fell company – meat pie for one, which in 1891 sickened thirteen individuals in Portsmouth, England; and for another, leg of pork, which killed three people in 1878.[22] In the latter instance blame fell on the place of purchase, where it was discovered that a clerk had kept the leg stored

> in a place which went by the name of a larder, under the stairs, communicating by a ventilator, on the one hand, with a dog

kennel, which had never been cleaned out, and, on the other hand, with a trapped gully, which was as foul as trapped gulleys usually are.[23]

Whether they involved kennels or 'trapped' gulleys, insanitary conditions often received blame for meat gone bad. The blame was not misplaced. American novelist Upton Sinclair famously exposed the reprehensible practices of the u.s. meatpacking industry in his 1906 novel *The Jungle*. 'There was never the least attention paid to what was cut up for sausage,' he wrote: 'there would come all the way back from Europe old sausage that had been rejected, and that was moldy and white.'[24] Yet rather than being discarded, he

Meat inspectors at work in Chicago's Swift & Co. meatpacking plant. Novelist Upton Sinclair and other reformers shone a light on the meatpacking industry's rampant abuses, which included neglect of proper sanitation. Meatpacking plants and their products teemed with all kinds of harmful microorganisms. Yet the reformers in the United States carried the day; pure food laws began entering the books by 1906.

continues, 'it would be dosed with borax and glycerine, and dumped into the hoppers, and made over again for home consumption.'[25] Newly made sausage had no more agreeable ingredients. In it went anything from 'meat that had tumbled out on the floor, in the dirt and sawdust, where the workers had tramped and spit uncounted billions of consumption germs' and 'dried dung of rats', to 'dirt and rust and old nails and stale water' and whatever else had found its way into the waste barrels.[26]

Sinclair's readers no doubt came to appreciate the sentiment behind Otto von Bismarck's quip, 'Laws are like sausages; it's better not to see how they are made.' Yet it was laws that finally made sausage safe for eating. The u.s. Pure Food and Drug Act of 1906 reined in the most egregious practices. And penned to aid manufacturers in compliance were such books as *Secrets of Meat Curing and Sausage Making*, which outlined practices for curing and fermenting meats under the new food laws. 'In its pages', the book's preface reads,

> are formulas and rules for the handling of all kinds of meat
> and the manufacture of all kinds of sausage which are the
> results of many years of experience as Packing House Experts
> and Chemists who have made a life-time study of the busi-
> ness in all its phases.[27]

Though the guidance of experts and chemists did much to advance clean, safe meatpacking, not until 1942 did industry find a way of reliably mass-producing sausages and other fermented meats. Scientists had previously isolated the bacterial strain responsible for dried and semi-dried sausages and hams, but it failed to perform under laboratory conditions. They therefore turned to isolating other kinds. *Pediococcus cerevisiae* turned out to be a good candidate. Not normally found in meat fermentations, it was introduced in the 1950s in the United States as the first meat

**WITH THE FREEZE-EM-PICKLE PROCESS AND
"A" AND "B" CONDIMENTINE ANYONE CAN
CURE MEAT AND MAKE GOOD SAUSAGE**

Early 20th-century print advertisement for a commercial sausage starter. Like other familiar fermented foods, cured meats and sausages came to be assimilated to scientific advances. Investigators isolated the bacteria crucial to fermentation, and these they turned over to businessmen for commercialization. The result was reliably safe if somewhat standardized and unremarkable offerings on market shelves.

starter culture. In the ensuing decades work was done to produce more viable *Lactobacillus* starter cultures.[28]

In the United States today, most fermented sausage starter cultures contain lactic acid bacteria alone. Sausage made with it ferments at a high temperature for a brief time, and certain varieties are subsequently cooked as an additional food safety measure. European sausage producers, meanwhile, take a different approach. They ferment sausage at a low temperature for a long time, using three kinds of microorganism – *Staphylococcus*, *Micrococcus* and *Kocuria*.[29] Differences in temperatures, times and microorganisms aside, factory-made sausage tends to lack the depth and complexity characteristic of small-scale production. Pepperoni and its cousin, summer sausage, for example, dominate the American market, and consumers are hard pressed to distinguish one brand from the other in terms of flavour.

Fortunately, production of fermented meats on a smaller scale has made a comeback. And thanks to government oversight, consumers may enjoy them safe in the knowledge that they will not kill them. The ingredients may still be unsavoury – hot dogs, for example, consist of mysterious bits and pieces – but the presence of an agency that has no financial interest in the sausage itself ensures that this once tasty but dangerous food may be eaten with confidence. Indeed, the triumph of the artisanal sausage may be considered a testament not only to the virtues of the financially disinterested bureaucrat, but also the right application of food science. For developments in hygiene and production have allowed sausage and other fermented meats to come into their own. Perhaps for the first time, we really would like to see how they are made.

# 8 A Different Relationship to Nourishment: *Fermented Foods Present and Future*

The key to health is fermentation, it turns out.
– Ruth Reichl[1]

FOR CENTURIES FERMENTED FOODS – bread, wine, beer, pickles, sausage, cheese – have nourished humanity through dearth and famine, the founding of ancient kingdoms and the building of industrial cities. They have fuelled trade and exploration. And they enabled millions of people to escape the pressing necessity of the moment. Fermentation, and food preservation generally, brought our forebears a bit of food security, which allowed them to concern themselves with things other than their next meal.

Some of those supramundane concerns were scientific in nature. Our investigations into the innermost recesses of nature – and ourselves – revealed entire realms of vanishingly small organisms living in our food and our viscera, the latter perhaps the most ideal fermentation vessel of all. It turns out that the human digestive system, one of the most complex ecosystems on earth, is home to trillions of such wee creatures.[2] Some 1,200 different species live in the guts of Americans, for example, nourishing their hosts even as they draw nourishment from them.[3]

The arrangement begins before we enter the world. As a foetus we take in microbes from our mother's amniotic fluid, placenta, lower intestine and birth canal – rich and varied microbiomes all.[4] Newly born, we add to our microbiome whenever we drink our mother's breast milk, which is similarly rich and varied.

We fully develop our gut microbiome by four years of age. Its population thenceforth remains fairly stable; microorganisms find a home somewhere along our digestive tract as they are introduced. Yet how long they make our gut a home depends on our diet and use of antibiotics.[5] Eighty per cent of a healthy adult's microbiota belongs to four dominant phyla: Gram-negative *Bacteroidetes*, Gram-negative *Proteobacteria*, Gram-positive *Actinobacteria* and Gram-negative *Firmicutes*.[6] Certain foods may cause shifts in the proportions. A diet high in fat and low in fibre, for example, promotes the growth of *Firmicutes* and *Proteobacteria*, whereas a low-fat, high-fibre diet favours *Bacteroidetes*.[7] A European study compared the microbiota of children who ate a typically Western diet to that of rural African children whose diet consisted of the fibre-rich foods traditionally eaten in their region. The African children's microbiota showed a greater presence of *Bacteroidetes*, along with bacteria belonging to the genera *Prevotella* and *Xylanibacter*. Perhaps unsurprisingly, fat-loving *Firmicutes* had a negligible presence.[8]

Whether a gut abounds in *Firmicutes* or *Bacteroidetes* may mean the difference between sickness and health. Dominant in the African children of the study were those microbes that maximize energy intake from dietary fibre and protect from inflammation and infection.[9] Yet a diet consisting solely of traditional foods is not necessarily prerequisite; the microbiota of each one of us acts in any number of ways that affect negatively or positively our overall health. Though it acts primarily to ferment into short-chain fatty acids such indigestible carbohydrates as cellulose, pectin, gums and resistant starches, it works other effects as well.[10] Research

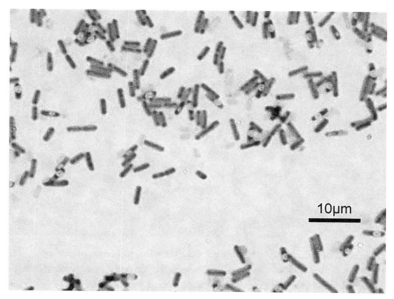

Colony of *Firmicutes*, bacteria that thrive in guts housed in individuals whose diet is high in fat and low in fibre.

has shown that our microbiome synthesizes vitamins B and K, develops and enhances the immune system, prevents allergies and protects against infections, heart disease and cancer. It can spur weight gain and it can spur weight loss.[11] It is akin to a vital organ and, as such, the state of its health means the difference between a long life of vitality with relative freedom from disease and a life foreshortened and plagued by ills.

Happily, we may snatch robust wellness from the jaws of ill health with relative ease. A few changes to a diet may alter a microbiome's composition in a day. In 2014 Jeff Leach, keeper of the Human Food Project website, made changes to his own. His experience, which he documented, took him from a diet low in carbohydrates and high in animal protein, to a diet high in both animal protein and fibre, and finally to a diet that was high-carb and meaty. When he began he had been living in New Orleans,

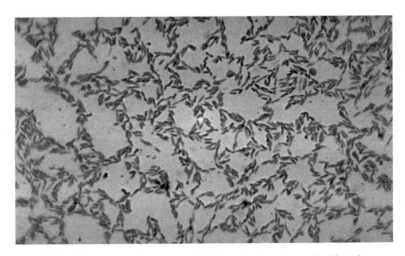

*Bacteroides biacutis*, one of the many gut flora beneficial to human health and digestion. Recent scientific investigations have expanded and refined understanding of the relationship between proper diet and a robust microbiome.

Louisiana, where he managed to get plenty of fibre in his otherwise meat-intensive diet. This changed with a move to western Texas, where his meat consumption continued as before but his fibre consumption did not. Stool samples revealed that during his tenure in Texas, Leach looked, as he wrote, 'like an entirely different person', microbially speaking. *Firmicutes* had dominated his gut microbiome in New Orleans. After some two or three weeks in the Lone Star State, however, *Bacteroidetes* had taken over. In decline also was *Bifidobacterium*, a bacterium plentiful in healthy guts. Waning levels of the latter microbe Leach attributed to the fact that he had ceased to eat onions, garlic, leeks and other foods rich in insoluble fibre. *Firmicutes* and *Bifidobacterium* represented just two casualties of Leach's move; the diversity among his gut microbes shrank by half in Texas. He writes that 'as Ecosystems 101 teaches us, a less diverse microbiota is less resilient to perturbations and may tip one closer to an unhealthy state.'[12] Leach had depopulated his gut to his greater peril.

As Élie Metchnikoff had discovered over a century before, lactic acid bacteria are especially health-promoting. A subspecies of *Lactobacillus delbrueckii* found in yoghurt and cheese, *Lactobacillus bulgaricus* reduces diarrhoea brought on by antibiotics and may help to relieve symptoms of lactose intolerance. Another bacterium in fermented dairy, *Lactobacillus casei*, stimulates the immune system, and, as studies have shown, may preserve survivors of bladder cancer from the disease's recurrence. *Lactobacillus johnsonii* not only reduces inflammation, but improves the response of individuals to oral vaccines and shrinks colonies of *Helicobacter pylori*, the microorganism responsible for stomach ulcers.[13]

This connection between health and the richness of one's microbiome has led to the development of seemingly innumerable probiotic products. Expected to reach U.S.$66 billion by 2024, the global market for probiotics includes food, beverages and nutraceuticals – foods whose benefit to health is more than nutritional (sometimes known as functional foods).[14] Consumers interested in gut health may now buy, among other foods, probiotic granola, margarine, brownie mix and orange juice.

Scientists may add even more foods to the array. Especially promising have been advances in probiotic adult beverages. Researchers in Brazil grew cultures of kefir – a dairy ferment hailing from the Caucasus that is similar to yoghurt – in molasses, which they in turn used in fermenting malt for beer.[15] In Singapore, researchers brewed beer with *Lactobacillus paracasei* L26, a lactic acid bacterium first isolated from the human intestine. Capable of neutralizing toxins and viruses and regulating the immune system, the *L. paracasei* fed on the sugars in the wort and produced a sharply tart beer. The researchers preserved it by way of a slow brew and an alcohol content kept to a low 3.5 per cent.[16]

Consumers who would rather not rely on dairy, beer or other culinary vehicles for these beneficial microbes also have options galore. Probiotic supplements boast strains for every ailment and

Modern supermarket aisle stocked with various functional foods. The increase in awareness of the role of gut microbiomes in human health has bred a concomitant increase in packaged foods suited to this role, sales of which are expected to soar into the billions in the next decade.

impressive numbers of live microorganisms, the latter measured in colony-forming units, or CFUs. Whether in the form of pills, powdered drink mixes, sweetened gummies and liquids, they promise '24/7 support' for everything from digestion to active lifestyles. And they tend to be prohibitively expensive.

The steep price of probiotic supplements is one consideration. Whether they truly work is another. By singling out one or two probiotic strains, we might be overlooking the nuances of how these microorganisms work within us. Some of their health effects are species-specific, while others are dose- and strain-specific.[17] Isolation of one or two bacterial strains for sale in pill or powder form may remove them from a wider, more complex scope of interactions on which their efficacy depends. Some health effects depend on the ingestion of a specific species or strain of microbe; others, on a specific dose. Not enough research has been done to substantiate blanket claims that the health benefits of one probiotic are also delivered by others.

And then there is the problem of dead bacteria, the presence of which manufacturers fail to account for in their products. If a product contains, say, only a few billion bacteria to begin with, die-off may not present a problem. Die-off in products containing hundreds of billions of bacteria, however, may prove harmful to individuals with compromised immune systems.[18]

These concerns can be reduced to the fact that we often fail to get our money's worth when we buy probiotic supplements. This became evident in an Israeli study. The study's nineteen subjects took probiotics that contained eleven of the most common bacterial strains. Of those nineteen subjects, only eight experienced a

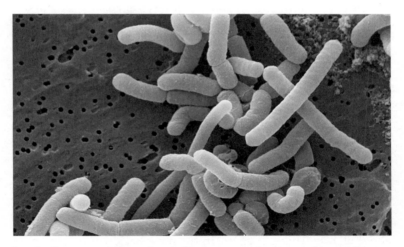

*Lactobacillus paracasei.* Researchers in Singapore recently attempted to enrich beer with the beneficial intestinal bacteria. The experiment proved a success once it was discovered that the beer must brew slowly. The result was a beverage that was not only healthy but appealingly tangy.

'notable colonization' of their gut. 'Surprisingly we found that many healthy volunteers were resistant,' said Professor Evan Segal of Tel Aviv's Weizmann Institute of Science, where the study was conducted. 'The probiotics couldn't colonise their tracts.' The number of people whose guts proved inhospitable to probiotics likely tracks with that of the larger population. From this arrived the conclusion that a one-size-fits-all approach does not work. Needed instead are supplement regimens tailored to individuals.[19] The health of our microbiome, it turns out, is dependent on factors wholly unique to our biology and our lifeworld. The bromide that each person is unique proves true in this case, and therefore mass-produced probiotics are seldom successful.

\* \* \*

The intimate relation between our microbiome and the world is why, when it comes to probiotics, diet trumps supplements. Only in real food may we find the diversity of pro- and prebiotics that can sustain health. The microbes first discovered by Metchnikoff had thrived in yoghurt, and it is to such naturally fermented foods that we must look if we want to stay healthy. Happily, selection has grown since Metchnikoff's day. On modern supermarket shelves appear some 3,500 types of fermented foods belonging to more than 250 categories.[20] Add fermented foods in developing countries, and the total grows higher. Such an existing variety makes a turn to highly processed functional foods unnecessary, if not ill-advised.

Indeed, we can learn much from food traditions that have endured. In many parts of the world, ferments are still considered integral to human health and well-being, serving to sustain life above all else. This is because, in the most basic sense, fermented food nourishes more than does unfermented food. Traditional ferments contain essential nutrients, and they protect those who consume them from disease and famine. A traditional sorghum

Pulque harvester plying his trade. The traditional fermented drink has sustained the peoples of Mexico for centuries, delivering them important B-complex vitamins.

beer provides riboflavin (vitamin B2) and niacin (vitamin B3) to people of southern Africa, keeping them from worse ravages of pellagra that their maize-dominated diet would otherwise leave them prone to. In West Africa, palm wine delivers needed vitamin B12 to people whose diet includes little meat. Thiamine (vitamin B1), niacin and riboflavin are contained in pulque, a plant-sap beer popular in parts of Mexico.[21]

Yet nourishment is only one benefit. Fermented foods protect in other, subtler ways. Bacterial pathogens do not survive long in a microbiome filled with beneficial bacteria, for the beneficial microbes outcompete the pathogenic for space and nutrients. Some beneficial bacteria even secrete chemicals that kill pathogens outright or coax a host's immune system into increasing its defences against the invaders.[22] Anyone who has suffered digestive upset while travelling inevitably wonders why the local population can eat and drink to no ill effect. The answer is in our microbiome. A tourist fed on a sterile diet of processed foods lacks the microflora necessary to kill the pathogenic bacteria present in a glass of water or slice of melon consumed abroad.

Strong communion with beneficial bacteria not only imparts health, it changes the way people inhabit the world. To ferment is to take nothing for granted. A store of kimchi or wheel of cheese is a hedge against an uncertain future, an acknowledgement that much remains beyond human control. And in those parts of the world where this truth is painfully manifest, fermented foods are all the more important. So-called famine, or survival, foods compose some 60 per cent of the Sudanese diet, for example. One such food is *kawal*, which is made from fermented and sun-dried leaves of the sicklepod senna. Rich in protein and other nutrients, kawal remains edible for years. These proved useful virtues during the famine that gripped Sudan from 1983 to 1985. As relief workers discovered, only those families that produced such fermented foods survived. Long tradition had established kawal as a reliable hedge. Families stop making it only when they feel they have savings enough for buying necessities in lean times.[23]

People accustomed to lean times allow little to go to waste, even in times of celebration. Indians deal with food left over during festivities in an ingenious way. The previous day's offerings, usually vegetarian, are layered in large earthenware pots, each layer salted before the next is added. They leave the layers to ferment until the festival's end, at which time they season them with oil, dried chillies, mustard leaves and curry leaves. The fermented, spiced mass they boil and serve hot.[24]

Peoples of Latin America show similar concern for food waste. Rinds left from processing pineapples serve as the key ingredient

Vendor selling tempeh bongkrek. A food long enjoyed in Indonesia, it is not without its perils. Should *Burkholderia gladioli* come to colonize it as it ferments, the individual unfortunate enough to be served it could fall deathly ill.

in vinegar. The rinds are added to containers filled with water, sugar and yeast. There they ferment until the mixture has become sufficiently acidic, a process that usually takes eight days or so.[25] In Indonesia, peanut and coconut presscake (the remains from oil extraction) are turned into *tempeh bongkrek*. The process involves inoculation of the presscake with filamentous *Rhizopus* fungi and culturing it in a banana leaf. When sliced and fried like its more familiar soy counterpart it is reportedly quite tasty. (However, risk does attend enjoyment of tempeh bongkrek: should it become infected by the bacterium *Burkholderia gladioli*, illness and death may follow its consumption.) And the ever-resourceful people of Sudan reclaim parts of game that would otherwise go to waste by making a dish known as *dodery*. They pulverize animal bones, place

Artisanal pickled vegetables for sale at a farmers' market in Brunswick, Maine. Contemporary health consciousness has led to renewed interest in foods made according to tradition. Handmade pickles and cured meats have joined craft beer and other comestibles in a veritable fermentation renaissance.

the bone bits in water and leave the vats to ferment. Three days later, the bone bits are removed, crushed into a paste and mixed with ash from burnt sorghum stalks before being returned to vats for another three or four days' fermentation. Ready batches of dodery are rolled into balls for storage or immediate consumption. Another Sudanese dish, *kaidu digla*, is made from the vertebrae of slain game. Pounded to a paste, fermented and rolled into balls for fermenting once more, it represents an essential source of protein and nutrients in an otherwise blandly farinaceous diet.[26]

Tempeh bongkrek, dodery, kaidu digla and foods like them share the common quality of rootedness in the cultures that brought them forth. Behind their invention lies no will to profit, only the will to endure. The relationship is mutually sustaining and, as such, is sustainable, whether in times of want or plenty. Food practices in more industrialized regions, on the other hand, have their genesis in market-oriented forms of thought, in which short-term profit trumps all other concerns. They allow us to feast today and tomorrow. But shall we find ourselves feasting the day after tomorrow?

Few of us can subsist entirely on home-made ferments. Yet where time and circumstance permit we ought to take up traditional ways of making and preserving food. Ferments made according to long tradition situate us, however temporarily, in a different relationship not only to nourishment and health, but to the world and those who must live in it. They remind us that food is not merely a biological necessity reducible to calories, vitamins, minerals and other useful elements. In their making we gain insight into a way of life that depends on values that cannot be bought or sold. For fermented foods recall to us the abiding truth that flourishes where there is diversity, balance and, perhaps most importantly, cooperation.

# References

Introduction Faithful Friends and Implacable Foes:
*The Nature and History of Our Relationship to Microbes*

1 Arthur Isaac Kendall, *Civilization and the Microbe* (Boston, MA, 1923), p. 223.
2 For a contemporary account of the Loch Maree poisonings, see Gerald Rowley Leighton, *Botulism and Food Preservation (The Loch Maree Tragedy)* (London, 1923). For a modern treatment, see Rosa K. Pawsey, *Case Studies in Food Microbiology for Food Safety and Quality* (London, 2007).
3 Leighton, *Botulism and Food Preservation*, pp. 193–4.
4 Thomas J. Montville and Karl R. Matthews, *Food Microbiology: An Introduction* (Washington, DC, 2005), pp. 187–98.
5 'Clostridium botulinum', at https://microbewiki.kenyon.edu, accessed 10 February 2018. The United States averages 25 cases of botulism per year, most of them occurring in Alaska.
6 Harvey A. Levenstein, *Fear of Food: A History of Why We Worry about What We Eat* (Chicago, IL, 2012), pp. 6–7.
7 Nancy Tomes, *The Gospel of Germs: Men, Women, and the Microbe in American Life* (Cambridge, MA, 1998), pp. 6–7.
8 Levenstein, *Fear of Food*, p. 12.
9 Harvey A. Levenstein, *Revolution at the Table: The Transformation of the American Diet* (New York, 1988), pp. 32–3.

10 Ibid., p. 35.

11 Ibid., p. 38.

12 Paul Clayton and Judith Rowbotham, 'An Unsuitable and Degraded Diet?, Part Three: Victorian Consumption Patterns and Their Health Benefits', *Journal of the Royal Society of Medicine*, CI/9 (2008), pp. 455–60.

13 Jean-Louis Flandrin, Massimo Montanari, Albert Sonnenfeld and Clarissa Botsford, *Food: A Culinary History from Antiquity to the Present* (New York, 2013), p. 495.

14 Bruno Latour, *The Pasteurization of France*, trans. Alan Sheridan and John Law (Cambridge, MA, 1993), p. 35.

15 Ed Yong, *I Contain Multitudes: The Microbes within Us and a Grander View of Life* (New York, 2018), p. 10.

16 H. G. Wells, *The Outline of History*, 2 vols (New York, 1921), vol. I, p. 12.

17 Yong, *I Contain Multitudes*, p. 9.

18 Ibid.

19 Stuart Hogg, *Essential Microbiology*, 2nd edn (Chichester, 2013), p. 345.

20 Yong, *I Contain Multitudes*, p. 10.

21 Percy F. Frankland, 'Microscopic Laborers and How They Serve Us', *English Illustrated Magazine*, VIII (1891), p. 117.

22 Thomas Hardy, *The Dynasts* (London, 1978), p. 88.

## 1 Laughter and Wild Play: *The Birth and Evolution of Fermented Drink*

1 Omar Khayyám, *Rubáiyát of Omar Khayyám: The Astronomer-Poet of Persia*, trans. Edward FitzGerald (New York, 1921), p. 163.

2 Nicholas P. Money, *The Rise of Yeast: How the Sugar Fungus Shaped Civilization* (New York, 2018), pp. 8–9.

3 Ibid.

4 S. A. Odunfa and O. B. Oywole, 'African Fermented Foods', in *Microbiology of Fermented Foods*, 2 vols, 2nd edn, ed. Brian J. B. Wood (London, 1998), vol. II, p. 727.

5 John W. Arthur, 'Brewing Beer: Status, Wealth, and Ceramic Use Alteration among the Gamo of South-western Ethiopia', *World Archaeology*, XXXIV/3 (2003), pp. 516–28.

6 Amaia Arranz-Otaegui et al., 'Archaeobotanical Evidence Reveals the Origins of Bread 14,400 Years Ago in Northeastern Jordan', *Proceedings of the National Academy of Sciences*, CXV/31 (2018), pp. 7925–30.

7  Amanda Borschel-Dan, '13,000-year-old Brewery Discovered in Israel, the Oldest in the World', *The Times of Israel*, 12 September 2018, www.timesofisrael.com.

8  Ian S. Hornsey, *A History of Beer and Brewing* (Cambridge, 2003), p. 86.

9  Ibid., p. 82.

10  Ibid., p. 89.

11  Ibid., pp. 110–11.

12  Max Nelson, *The Barbarian's Beverage: A History of Beer in Ancient Europe* (London, 2005), p. 10.

13  Kenneth F. Kiple and Kriemhild Coneè Ornelas, eds, *The Cambridge World History of Food*, 2 vols (Cambridge, 2000), vol. 1, pp. 730–40.

14  Edward Hyams, *Dionysus: A Social History of the Wine Vine* (New York, 1965), pp. 36–7.

15  Ian Tattersall and Rob DeSalle, *A Natural History of Wine* (New Haven, CT, 2015), p. 12.

16  Hyams, *Dionysus*, p. 65.

17  Nelson, *Barbarian's Beverage*, p. 72.

18  Ibid., p. 35.

19  Tattersall and DeSalle, *Natural History of Wine*, p. 15.

20  William Younger, *Gods, Men, and Wine* (Cleveland, OH, 1966), p. 131.

21  Ibid., p. 192.

22  Hyams, *Dionysus*, p. 82.

23  Virgil, *The Eclogues; The Georgics*, trans. C. Day Lewis (New York, 1999), p. 83.

24  Younger, *Gods, Men, and Wine*, p. 187.

25  Henry H. Work, *The Shape of Wine: Its Packaging Evolution* (London, 2018), p. 121.

26  Younger, *Gods, Men, and Wine*, p. 187.

27  Robert Sechrist, *Planet of the Grapes: A Geography of Wine* (Santa Barbara, CA, 2017), p. 12.

28  Zhengping Li, *Chinese Wine* (Cambridge, 2011), pp. 1–2.

29  Ibid., p. 5.

30  Ibid., p. 3.

31  Kiple and Ornelas, *Cambridge World History of Food*, p. 621.

32  Hornsey, *History of Beer and Brewing*, p. 284.

33  Ibid., p. 289.

34  Kiple and Ornelas, *Cambridge World History of Food*, p. 619.

35  Ibid., p. 622.

36 Richard W. Unger, *A History of Brewing in Holland 900–1900: Economy, Technology and the State* (Leiden, 2001), p. 377.

37 Ibid., p. 29.

38 Ibid., p. 69.

39 Ibid.

40 Ibid., p. 72.

41 Ibid., p. 89.

42 Simon Schama, *The Embarrassment of Riches: An Interpretation of Dutch Culture in the Golden Age* (Berkeley, CA, 1988), p. 172.

43 Unger, *History of Brewing in Holland*, p. 125.

44 Ibid.

45 Ibid., pp. 128–9.

46 Ibid., p. 124.

47 Ibid., p. 125.

48 Ibid., p. 113.

49 Ibid., p. 115.

50 Ibid., p. 110.

51 Hornsey, *History of Beer and Brewing*, p. 621.

52 Ibid.

## 2 'Un Grand Progrès': The Industrialization of Fermented Drink

1 R. E. Egerton-Warburton, *Poems, Epigrams and Sonnets* (London, 1877), p. 93.

2 Patrice Debré, *Louis Pasteur*, trans. Elborg Forster (Baltimore, MD, 1998), pp. 226–9.

3 Ibid.

4 Louise Robbins, *Louis Pasteur and the Hidden World of Microbes* (New York, 2001), p. 50.

5 Debré, *Louis Pasteur*, p. 219.

6 John Farley and Gerald L. Geison, 'Science, Politics and Spontaneous Generation in Nineteenth-century France', *Bulletin of the History of Medicine*, XLVIII/2 (1974), pp. 161–98.

7 Debré, *Louis Pasteur*, p. 220.

8 Ibid., p. 7.

9 Ibid., pp. 230–31.

10 René Vallery-Radot, *Louis Pasteur: His Life and Labours*, trans. Lady Claud Hamilton (New York, 1891), p. 120.

11  Ibid., p. 121.

12  Debré, *Louis Pasteur*, p. 89.

13  Ibid., p. 90.

14  Ibid., p. 92.

15  Ibid., p. 91.

16  Ibid., p. 240.

17  William T. Brannt, *A Practical Treatise on the Manufacture of Vinegar and Acetates, Cider, and Fruit-wines* (Philadelphia, PA, 1890), p. 22.

18  Debré, *Louis Pasteur*, p. 239.

19  Ibid., p. 241.

20  R. Wahl, 'Pasteur's "Studies on Beer" the Foundation of Medical Science', *American Brewers' Review* (May 1914), pp. 199–201.

21  Much of this information on Hansen appears in Louise Crane, 'Legends of Brewing: Emil Christian Hansen', www.beer52.com, 6 December 2017.

22  Ian S. Hornsey, *A History of Beer and Brewing* (Cambridge, 2003), p. 403.

23  Ibid., p. 412.

24  Ibid.

25  Ibid., p. 413.

26  Ibid.

27  Ibid.

28  Ibid., p. 409.

29  Ibid.

30  Ibid.

31  Ibid.

32  Ibid., p. 410.

33  Ibid.

34  Ibid., p. 411.

35  Ibid.

36  Ibid., p. 410.

37  Ibid., p. 415.

38  James A. Barnett and Linda Barnett, *Yeast Research: A Historical Overview* (Washington, DC, 2011), p. 19.

39  Louis Pasteur, *Studies on Fermentation: The Diseases of Beer, Their Causes, and the Means of Preventing Them*, trans. Frank Faulkner and D. Constable Robb (London, 1879), p. 23.

40  Ibid., p. 26.

41 Barnett and Barnett, *Yeast Research*, p. 19.
42 Thomas Dale Brock, *Robert Koch: A Life in Medicine and Bacteriology*, 2nd edn (Washington, DC, 1999), p. 94.
43 Crane, 'Legends of Brewing'.
44 Ibid.
45 Barnett and Barnett, *Yeast Research*, p. 29.
46 Brock, *Robert Koch*, p. 100.
47 Ibid., p. 101.
48 Ibid., p. 116.
49 Ibid., p. 97.
50 Ibid., p. 98.
51 Ibid., p. 97.
52 Barnett and Barnett, *Yeast Research*, p. 29.
53 Ibid.
54 Crane, 'Legends of Brewing'.
55 Valdemar Meisen, ed., *Prominent Danish Scientists through the Ages, with Facsimiles from Their Works*, trans. Hans Andersen (Copenhagen, 1932), p. 162.
56 Crane, 'Legends of Brewing'.
57 Ibid.
58 Ibid.
59 Kenneth F. Kiple and Kriemhild Coneè Ornelas, eds, *The Cambridge World History of Food*, 2 vols (Cambridge, 2000), vol. 1, p. 624.

3 'Oven Worship': *Bread and Its Various Preparations from Earliest Antiquity to the Present*

1 Lewis Carroll, *Through the Looking-glass* (Oxford, 1998), p. 164.
2 James A. Barnett and Linda Barnett, *Yeast Research: A Historical Overview* (Washington, DC, 2011), p. 29.
3 Much of the information on Horsford I have taken from Linda Civitello, *Baking Powder Wars: The Cutthroat Food Fight That Revolutionized Cooking* (Urbana, IL, 2017), pp. 36–46.
4 Eben Horsford, *The Theory and Art of Bread-making: A New Process without the Use of Ferment* (Cambridge, MA, 1861), p. 11.
5 *The Royal Baker and Pastry Cook: A Manual of Practical Cookery* (New York, 1902), pp. 1–2.

6 Nicholas P. Money, *The Rise of Yeast: How the Sugar Fungus Shaped Civilization* (New York, 2018), pp. 129–30.

7 Ibid., p. 11.

8 Ibid., p. 146.

9 Ibid., pp. 147–9.

10 Constantine John Alexopoulos, Charles W. Mims and Meredith Blackwell, *Introductory Mycology*, 4th edn (New York, 1996), p. 276.

11 B. Cordell and J. McCarthy, 'A Case Study of Gut Fermentation Syndrome (Auto-brewery) with Saccharomyces Cerevisiae as the Causative Organism', *International Journal of Clinical Medicine*, IV/7 (2013), pp. 309–12.

12 Harold McGee, *On Food and Cooking: The Science and Lore of the Kitchen* (New York, 1988), p. 275.

13 John S. Marchant, Bryan G. Reuben and Joan P. Alcock, *Bread: A Slice of History* (Stroud, 2010), pp. 19–20.

14 Ibid., p. 20.

15 Heinrich Eduard Jacob, *Six Thousand Years of Bread: Its Holy and Unholy History* (Garden City, NY, 1944), pp. 31–2.

16 Marchant, Reuben and Alcock, *Bread*, pp. 26–7.

17 Jacob, *Six Thousand Years of Bread*, p. 77.

18 Ibid., pp. 124–5.

19 Marchant, Reuben and Alcock, *Bread*, pp. 32–3.

20 Jacob, *Six Thousand Years of Bread*, p. 136.

21 Ibid., p. 138.

22 Ibid., pp. 137–8.

23 Quoted in Elizabeth David, *English Bread and Yeast Cookery* (New York, 1980), pp. 181–2.

24 Emil Braun, *The Baker's Book: A Practical Hand Book of All the Baking Industries in All Countries*, 2 vols (New York, 1903), vol. II, pp. 556–7.

25 R. Sankaran, 'Fermented Foods of the Indian Subcontinent', in *Microbiology of Fermented Foods*, 2 vols, 2nd edn, ed. Brian J. B. Wood (London, 1998), vol. II, pp. 765–8.

26 S. A. Odunfa and O. B. Oyewole. 'African Fermented Foods', in *Microbiology of Fermented Foods*, ed. Wood, vol. II, pp. 723–4.

27 Civitello, *Baking Powder Wars*, p. 6.

28 Ibid., p. 20.

29 Ibid.

30 Ibid., p. 29.

31 David Graeber, *Bullshit Jobs* (New York, 2018), p. 91.

32 Braun, *Baker's Book*, p. 562.

33 McGee, *On Food and Cooking*, p. 281.

34 William A. Alcott, George W. Light and Benjamin Bradley, *The Young House-keeper, or Thoughts on Food and Cookery* (Boston, MA, 1838), p. 130.

35 McGee, *On Food and Cooking*, p. 281.

36 Isabella Beeton, *Mrs Beeton's Household Management* (Ware, 2006), p. 784.

37 Civitello, *Baking Powder Wars*, p. 57.

38 Marchant, Reuben and Alcock, *Bread*, p. 70.

39 Ibid., pp. 112–13.

40 Ibid., pp. 139–40.

41 David, *English Bread and Yeast Cookery*, p. 195.

42 Siegfried Giedion, *Mechanization Takes Command: A Contribution to Anonymous History* (New York, 1955), pp. 196–8.

43 Ibid., p. 201.

44 Civitello, *Baking Powder Wars*, p. 30.

45 K. Katina et al., 'Potential of Sourdough for Healthier Cereal Products', *Trends in Food Science and Technology*, XVI/1–3 (2005), pp. 104–12.

46 Raffaella Di Cagno et al., 'Sourdough Bread Made from Wheat and Nontoxic Flours and Started with Selected Lactobacilli Is Tolerated in Celiac Sprue Patients', *Applied and Environmental Microbiology*, LXX/2 (2004), p. 1088.

## 4 A Sometimes Dicey Duality: *Fungi and Food*

1 Clyde M. Christensen, *The Molds and Man: An Introduction to the Fungi*, 3rd edn (Minneapolis, MN, 1965), p. 5.

2 Ibid., p. 186.

3 Michael Tunick, *The Science of Cheese* (New York, 2014), p. 109.

4 George W. Hudler, *Magical Mushrooms, Mischievous Molds* (Princeton, NJ, 2000), pp. 139–40.

5 William Shurtleff and Akiko Aoyagi, *History of Koji – Grains and/ or Soybeans Enrobed with a Mold Culture (300 BCE to 2012): Extensively Annotated Bibliography and Sourcebook* (Lafayette, CA, 2012), pp. 5–6.

6 Ibid., pp. 8–9.

7 Thomas J. Montville and Karl R. Matthews, *Food Microbiology: An Introduction* (Washington, DC, 2005), p. 279.

8 Ibid., pp. 278–9.

9 J. W. Bennett and M. Klich, 'Mycotoxins', *Clinical Microbiology Reviews*, XVI/3 (2003), pp. 497–516.

10 Stuart Hogg, *Essential Microbiology*, 2nd edn (Chichester, 2013), p. 203.

11 Hudler, *Magical Mushrooms, Mischievous Molds*, p. 19.

12 M. L. Smith, J. N. Bruhn and J. A. Anderson, 'The Fungus *Armillaria Bulbosa* Is among the Largest and Oldest Living Organisms', *Nature*, CCCLVI/6368 (1992), pp. 428–31.

13 Vincent S.F.T. Merckx, ed., *Mycoheterotrophy: The Biology of Plants Living on Fungi* (New York, 2013), p. v.

14 Thomas N. Taylor, Michael Krings and Edith L. Taylor, *Fossil Fungi* (London, 2015), p. 1.

15 Hudler, *Magical Mushrooms, Mischievous Molds*, pp. 217–19.

16 Christensen, *Molds and Man*, p. 51.

17 Hogg, *Essential Microbiology*, p. 205.

18 Ibid.

19 Hudler, *Magical Mushrooms*, p. 16.

20 Nicholas P. Money, *The Triumph of the Fungi: A Rotten History* (New York, 2007), pp. 121–7.

21 Quoted ibid., p. 126.

22 Ibid., p. 127.

23 Miles Joseph Berkeley, 'Observations, Botanical and Physiological, on the Potato Murrain', *Journal of the Horticultural Society of London*, 2 vols (London, 1846), vol. I, pp. 23–4.

24 Ibid., p. 24.

25 Money, *Triumph of the Fungi*, p. 120.

26 Robert Thatcher Rolfe and F. W. Rolfe, *The Romance of the Fungus World: An Account of Fungus Life in Its Numerous Guises, Both Real and Legendary* (London, 1925), p. 93.

27 Eden Phillpotts, *Children of the Mist* (New York, 1898), pp. 439–40.

28 Quoted in G. C. Ainsworth, *Introduction to the History of Mycology* (New York, 1976), p. 13.

29 Quoted ibid., p. 12.

30 Frank Dugan, *Fungi in the Ancient World: How Mushrooms, Mildews, Molds, and Yeast Shaped the Early Civilizations of Europe, the Mediterranean, and the Near East* (St Paul, MN, 2008), pp. 84–5.

31  Quoted in William Houghton, 'Notices of Fungi in Greek and Latin Authors', *Annals and Magazine of Natural History*, xv/5 (1885), p. 26.

32  Quoted ibid., p. 27.

33  Quoted ibid.

34  Quoted ibid., p. 28.

35  Quoted ibid.

36  Ainsworth, *History of Mycology*, p. 183.

37  Ibid.

38  Dugan, *Fungi in the Ancient World*, p. 58.

39  Ibid., p. 103.

40  Ainsworth, *History of Mycology*, p. 140.

41  R. C. Cooke, *Fungi, Man and His Environment* (London, 1997), pp. 106–8.

42  Ibid., p. 106.

43  Ibid., p. 108.

44  Quoted in Ainsworth, *History of Mycology*, p. 15.

45  Quoted ibid., p. 58.

46  Quoted ibid., p. 15.

47  Quoted ibid., pp. 164–5.

48  Quoted ibid., p. 166.

49  Ibid.

50  Ibid., p. 170.

51  Ibid., pp. 270–71.

52  Carol Pineda et al., 'Maternal Sepsis, Chorioamnionitis, and Congenital *Candida Kefyr* Infection in Premature Twins', *Pediatric Infectious Disease Journal*, xxxi/3 (2012), pp. 320–22.

53  Marianne Martinello et al., '"We Are What We Eat!" Invasive Intestinal Mucormycosis: A Case Report and Review of the Literature', *Medical Mycology Case Reports*, i/i (2012), pp. 52–5.

5 One of the Miracles of Everyday Life: *The Origins, Power and Fortunes of Vegetable Ferments*

1  Henry Mayhew, *German Life and Manners as Seen in Saxony at the Present Day*, 2 vols (London, 1864), vol. i, p. 174.

2  James Cook, *Captain Cook's Voyages round the World*, ed. M. B. Synge (London, 1900), p. 32.

3  Stephen K. Brown, *Scurvy: How a Surgeon, a Mariner, and a Gentleman Solve the Greatest Medical Mystery of the Age of Sail* (New York, 2003), pp. 17–18.

4  John R. Hale, *Age of Exploration* (New York, 1974), p. 83.

5  Elena Molokhovets, *Classic Russian Cooking: Elena Molokhovets' A Gift to Young Housewives*, trans. Joyce Toomre (Bloomington, IN, 1992), p. 16.

6  Wilhelm Holzapfel and Brian J. B. Wood, *Lactic Acid Bacteria: Biodiversity and Taxonomy* (Hoboken, NJ, 2014), pp. 44–6.

7  Ibid.

8  Cornell University Milk Quality Improvement Program, 'Lactic Acid Bacteria – Homofermentative and Heterofermentative', *Dairy Food Science Notes* (October 2008), p. 1.

9  Ibid.

10 Edward Farnworth, ed., *Handbook of Fermented Functional Foods* (Boca Raton, FL, 2003), pp. 349–50.

11 Lanming Chen, 'Diversity of Lactic Acid Bacteria in Chinese Traditional Fermented Foods', in *Beneficial Microbes in Fermented and Functional Foods*, ed. V. Ravishankar Rai and Jamuna A. Bai (Boca Raton, FL, 2015), pp. 3–14.

12 Jyoti Prakash Tamang and Kasipathy Kailasapathy, eds, *Fermented Foods and Beverages of the World* (Boca Raton, FL, 2010), p. 8.

13 Charles W. Bamforth and Robert E. Ward, eds, *The Oxford Handbook of Food Fermentations* (New York, 2014), p. 423.

14 Tamang and Kailasapathy, *Fermented Foods and Beverages*, p. 10.

15 Ibid., p. 9.

16 Sook-ja Soon, *Good Morning, Kimchi!* (Seoul, 2005), p. 10.

17 Tamang and Kailasapathy, *Fermented Foods and Beverages*, pp. 166–7.

18 Bamforth and Ward, *Oxford Handbook of Food Fermentations*, pp. 425–6.

19 Ibid., p. 427.

20 Ibid., pp. 431–2.

21 Chinua Achebe, *Things Fall Apart* (Oxford, 1996), p. 116.

22 Keith Steinkraus, ed., *Handbook of Indigenous Fermented Foods*, 2nd edn (New York, 1996), pp. 358–9.

23 Harvey A. Levenstein, *Revolution at the Table: The Transformation of the American Diet* (New York, 1988), p. 37.

24 Ibid., p. 36.

25 Thomas S. Blair, *Public Hygiene*, 2 vols (Boston, MA, 1911), vol. II, p. 457.
26 Mary B. Hughes, *Everywoman's Canning Book: The ABC of Safe Home Canning and Preserving by the Cold Pack Method* (Boston, MA, 1918), p. 4.

### 6 Microbes Working Their Magic: *Cheese, Yoghurt and Other Dairy Ferments*

1 Don Marquis, *The Best of Archy and Mehitabel*, ed. George Herriman (New York, 2011), p. 151.
2 Deborah M. Valenze, *Milk: A Local and Global History* (New Haven, CT, 2011), pp. 212–13.
3 Ana Lúcia Barretto Penna et al., 'Overview of the Functional Lactic Acid Bacteria in Fermented Milk Products', in *Beneficial Microbes in Fermented and Functional Foods*, ed. V. Ravishankar Rai and Jamuna A. Bai (Boca Raton, FL, 2015), pp. 113–48.
4 Julie Dunne et al., 'First Dairying in Green Saharan Africa in the Fifth Millennium BC', *Nature*, CDLXXXVI/7403 (2012), pp. 390–94.
5 Frederick J. Simoons, 'The Antiquity of Dairying in Asia and Africa', *Geographical Review*, LXI/3 (1971), pp. 431–9.
6 Andrea S. Wiley, *Cultures of Milk* (Cambridge, MA, 2014), p. 57.
7 Ibid., p. 58.
8 Ibid., p. 30.
9 Mélanie Salque et al., 'Earliest Evidence for Cheese Making in the Sixth Millennium BC in Northern Europe', *Nature*, CDXCIII/7433 (2013), pp. 522–5.
10 Catherine Donnelly, ed., *The Oxford Companion to Cheese* (New York, 2016), p. 247.
11 Traci Watson, 'Great Gouda! World's Oldest Cheese Found – on Mummies', *USA Today*, 25 February 2014, www.usatoday.com.
12 Aristotle, 'Generation of Animals', in *Complete Works of Aristotle*, ed. Jonathan Barnes, 2 vols (Princeton, NJ, 1984), vol. I, pp. 1111–218.
13 Homer, *The Odyssey*, trans. George Herbert Palmer (Boston, MA, 1921), p. 130.
14 L. Junius Moderatus Columella, *Of Husbandry* (London, 1745), pp. 324–5.
15 Pliny the Elder, *The Natural History of Pliny*, trans. John Bostock and H. T. Riley, 6 vols (London, 1855), vol. III, p. 85.

16  Valenze, *Milk*, p. 26.

17  Ibid., pp. 51–2.

18  Ibid., pp. 83–5.

19  Ibid., p. 92.

20  John Ray, *Travels through the Low-Countries: Germany, Italy and France*, 2 vols (London, 1738), vol. I, p. 44.

21  Valenze, *Milk*, p. 89.

22  Donnelly, *Oxford Companion to Cheese*, p. 723.

23  Robert Hooke, *Micrographia, or, Some Physiological Descriptions of Minute Bodies Made by Magnifying Glasses, with Observations and Inquiries Thereupon* (Lincolnwood, IL, 1987), p. 125.

24  Juliet Harbutt, ed., *World Cheese Book* (London, 2009), p. 7.

25  Paul S. Kindstedt, *Cheese and Culture: A History of Cheese and Its Place in Western Civilization* (White River Junction, VT, 2012), pp. 204–5.

26  Ibid., pp. 206–7.

27  Ibid., p. 209.

28  Ibid., pp. 206–7.

29  Charles Thom and Walter W. Fisk, *The Book of Cheese* (New York, 1918), pp. 2–3.

30  Kenneth B. Raper, 'Charles Thom 1872–1956', *Journal of Bacteriology*, LXXIV/6 (1956), pp. 725–7.

31  Desmond K. O'Toole, 'The Origin of Single Strain Starter Culture Usage for Commercial Cheddar Cheesemaking', *International Journal of Dairy Technology*, LVII/1 (2004), pp. 53–5.

32  Clotaire Rapaille, *The Culture Code: An Ingenious Way to Understand Why People around the World Buy and Live as They Do* (New York, 2006), p. 25.

33  Nicholas P. Money, *The Rise of Yeast: How the Sugar Fungus Shaped Civilization* (New York, 2018), p. 162.

34  Élie Metchnikoff, *The Prolongation of Life: Optimistic Studies*, ed. P. Chalmers Mitchell (New York, 1908), p. 165.

35  Patrice Debré, *Louis Pasteur*, trans. Elborg Forster (Baltimore, MD, 1998), pp. 99–100.

36  Ibid., p. 99.

37  Wilhelm Holzapfel and Brian J. B. Wood, *Lactic Acid Bacteria: Biodiversity and Taxonomy* (Hoboken, NJ, 2014), pp. 7–8.

38  Metchnikoff, *Prolongation of Life*, p. 166.

39  Ibid., p. 176.

40 Ibid., p. 171.
41 Evelyn Waugh, *A Handful of Dust* (Harmondsworth, 1951), p. 7.
42 Gabrichidze Manana, '"In Soviet Georgia" – the Story Behind the Cult Yogurt Ad', *Georgian Journal*, 18 April 2015, www.georgianjournal.ge.
43 Ibid.
44 Transparency Market Research, 'Kefir Market: Kefir's Ability to Boost Immunity, Bone Strength, and Digestion Leads to Its Sales', 21 August 2018, www.openPR.com.

7 Tasty but Dangerous: *The Virtues and Risks of Sausage and Fermented Meats*

1 Émile Zola, *The Fat and the Thin*, trans. Ernest Alfred Vizetelly (New York, 2005), p. 49.
2 Waverley Root, *Food: An Authoritative, Visual History and Dictionary of the Foods of the World* (New York, 1980), p. 479.
3 Ruth Blasco et al., 'Bone Marrow Storage and Delayed Consumption at Middle Pleistocene Qesem Cave, Israel (420 to 200 ka)', *Science Advances*, v/10 (2019), pp. 1–12.
4 G. Campbell-Platt and P. E. Cook. *Fermented Meats* (Boston, MA, 1995), p. 53.
5 Homer, *The Odyssey*, trans. George Herbert Palmer (Boston, MA, 1921), pp. 310–11.
6 Campbell-Platt and Cook, *Fermented Meats*, p. 15.
7 Ibid., p. 147.
8 Fidel Toldrá, ed., *Handbook of Fermented Meat and Poultry*, 2nd edn (Hoboken, NJ, 2014), p. 13.
9 Ibid., p. 373.
10 Joan P. Alcock, 'Fundolus or Botulus: Sausages in the Classical World', in *Cured, Fermented and Smoked Foods: Proceedings of the Oxford Symposium on Food and Cookery 2010*, ed. Helen Saberi (Totnes, 2011), pp. 44–5.
11 Quoted ibid., p. 40.
12 Ibid., pp. 43–4.
13 Toldrá, *Fermented Meat and Poultry*, p. 371.
14 Ibid., p. 373.
15 Ibid., p. 374.

16 Jyoti Prakash Tamang and Kasipathy Kailasapathy, eds, *Fermented Foods and Beverages of the World* (Boca Raton, FL, 2010), pp. 294–5.
17 Ibid., p. 294.
18 Kofi Manso Essuman, *Fermented Fish in Africa: A Study on Processing, Marketing and Consumption* (Rome, 1993), pp. 29–30.
19 Donald Emmeluth, *Botulism*, 2nd edn (New York, 2010), pp. 16–17.
20 Alexander Wynter Blyth, *Poisons, Their Effects and Detection: A Manual for the Use of Analytical Chemists and Experts* (London, 1884), pp. 476–7.
21 Ibid., p. 477.
22 Alexander Wynter Blyth, *Poisons, Their Effects and Detection: A Manual for the Use of Analytical Chemists and Experts*, 3rd edn (London, 1895), p. 508.
23 George Vivian Poore, *A Treatise on Medical Jurisprudence* (London, 1901), pp. 227–8.
24 Upton Sinclair, *The Jungle* (New York, 1906), p. 161.
25 Ibid., pp. 161–2.
26 Ibid., p. 162.
27 *Secrets of Meat Curing and Sausage Making*, 5th edn (Chicago, IL, 1922), p. 19.
28 Robert W. Hutkins, *Microbiology and Technology of Fermented Foods* (Ames, IA, 2006), pp. 212–13.
29 Ibid., p. 218.

8 A Different Relationship to Nourishment: *Fermented Foods Present and Future*

1 Ruth Reichl, 'Michael Pollan and Ruth Reichl Hash out the Food Revolution', *Smithsonian*, June 2013, www.smithsonianmag.com.
2 Jyoti Prakash Tamang, *Health Benefits of Fermented Foods and Beverages* (Hoboken, NJ, 2015), pp. 198–9.
3 Justin Sonnenburg and Erica Sonnenburg, *The Good Gut: Taking Control of Your Weight, Your Mood, and Your Long-term Health* (New York, 2015), p. 5.
4 Tamang, *Health Benefits*, p. 199.
5 Ibid.
6 Ibid., pp. 199–200.
7 Ibid., p. 201.
8 Ibid., p. 202.

9 Ibid., pp. 202–3.

10 Ibid., p. 208.

11 Ibid., pp. 205–7.

12 Jeff Leach, 'Going Feral: My One-year Journey to Acquire the Healthiest Gut Microbiome in the World (You Heard Me!)', 19 January 2014, http://humanfoodproject.com.

13 Tamang, *Health Benefits*, pp. 237–9.

14 Research and Markets, 'Probiotics Market Analysis to Reach $66 Billion by 2024 – Growing Preference for Functional Foods to Curb Health Disorders', 28 November 2016, www.businesswire.com.

15 Kamila Leite Rodrigues et al., 'A Novel Beer Fermented by Kefir Enhances Anti-inflammatory and Anti-ulcerogenic Activities Found Isolated in Its Constituents', *Journal of Functional Foods*, XXI (2016), pp. 58–69.

16 Mike Pomranz, 'Probiotic Beer Is Here to Help Your Gut (If Not Your Liver)', *Food & Wine*, 29 June 2017, www.foodandwine.com.

17 Claudio De Simone, 'The Unregulated Probiotic Market', *Clinical Gastroenterology and Hepatology*, XVII/5 (2019), pp. 809–17.

18 Ibid., pp. 811–13.

19 Victoria Allen, 'Why Probiotic Yoghurt May Be Pointless for Half of Us', *Daily Mail*, 7 September 2018, www.dailymail.co.uk.

20 S. S. Deshpande et al., *Fermented Grain Legumes, Seeds and Nuts: A Global Perspective* (Rome, 2000), pp. 10–11.

21 Mike Battcock and Sue Azam-Ali, *Fermented Fruits and Vegetables: A Global Perspective* (Delhi, 1998), pp. 39–40.

22 Sonnenburg and Sonnenburg, *Good Gut*, p. 165.

23 Battcock and Azam-Ali, *Fermented Fruits and Vegetables*, pp. 69–70.

24 R. Sankaran, 'Fermented Foods of the Indian Subcontinent', in *Microbiology of Fermented Foods*, 2 vols, 2nd edn, ed. Brian J. B. Wood (Boston, MA, 1998), vol. II, pp. 780–81.

25 Battcock and Azam-Ali, *Fermented Fruits and Vegetables*, pp. 72–3.

26 Ibid., p. 9.

# Select Bibliography

Bamforth, Charles W., and Robert E. Ward, eds, *The Oxford Handbook of Food Fermentations* (New York, 2014)

Barnett, James A., and Linda Barnett, *Yeast Research: A Historical Overview* (Washington, DC, 2011)

Battcock, Mike, and Sue Azam-Ali, *Fermented Fruits and Vegetables: A Global Perspective* (Delhi, 1998)

Campbell-Platt, G., and P. E. Cook, *Fermented Meats* (Boston, MA, 1995)

Christensen, Clyde M., *The Molds and Man: An Introduction to the Fungi*, 3rd edn (Minneapolis, MN, 1965)

Civitello, Linda, *Baking Powder Wars: The Cutthroat Food Fight That Revolutionized Cooking* (Urbana, IL, 2017)

David, Elizabeth, *English Bread and Yeast Cookery* (New York, 1980)

Debré, Patrice, *Louis Pasteur*, trans. Elborg Forster (Baltimore, MD, 1998)

Deshpande, S. S., et al., *Fermented Grain Legumes, Seeds and Nuts: A Global Perspective* (Rome, 2000)

Donnelly, Catherine, ed., *The Oxford Companion to Cheese* (New York, 2016)

Dugan, Frank, *Fungi in the Ancient World: How Mushrooms, Mildews, Molds, and Yeast Shaped the Early Civilizations of Europe, the Mediterranean, and the Near East* (St Paul, MN, 2008)

Essuman, Kofi Manso, *Fermented Fish in Africa: A Study on Processing, Marketing and Consumption* (Rome, 1993)

Flandrin, Jean-Louis, Massimo Montanari, Albert Sonnenfeld and Clarissa Botsford, *Food: A Culinary History from Antiquity to the Present* (New York, 2013)

Holzapfel, Wilhelm, and Brian J. B. Wood, *Lactic Acid Bacteria: Biodiversity and Taxonomy* (Hoboken, NJ, 2014)

Hornsey, Ian S., *A History of Beer and Brewing* (Cambridge, 2003)

Horsford, Eben, *The Theory and Art of Bread-making: A New Process without the Use of Ferment* (Cambridge, MA, 1861)

Hudler, George W., *Magical Mushrooms, Mischievous Molds* (Princeton, NJ, 2000)

Hutkins, Robert W., *Microbiology and Technology of Fermented Foods* (Ames, IA, 2006)

Jacob, Heinrich Eduard, *Six Thousand Years of Bread: Its Holy and Unholy History* (Garden City, NY, 1944)

Katz, Sandor Ellix, *Wild Fermentation: The Flavor, Nutrition, and Craft of Live-culture Foods* (White River Junction, VT, 2016)

Kindstedt, Paul S., *Cheese and Culture: A History of Cheese and Its Place in Western Civilization* (White River Junction, VT, 2012)

Latour, Bruno, *The Pasteurization of France*, trans. Alan Sheridan and John Law (Cambridge, MA, 1993)

Levenstein, Harvey A., *Revolution at the Table: The Transformation of the American Diet* (New York, 1988)

Li, Zhengping, *Chinese Wine* (Cambridge, 2011)

Marchant, John S., Bryan G. Reuben and Joan P. Alcock, *Bread: A Slice of History* (Stroud, 2010)

Money, Nicholas P., *The Rise of Yeast: How the Sugar Fungus Shaped Civilization* (New York, 2018)

—, *The Triumph of the Fungi: A Rotten History* (New York, 2007)

Montville, Thomas J., and Karl R. Matthews, *Food Microbiology: An Introduction* (Washington, DC, 2005)

Nelson, Max, *The Barbarian's Beverage: A History of Beer in Ancient Europe* (London, 2005)

Oliver, Garrett, *The Oxford Companion to Beer* (New York, 2012)

Pasteur, Louis, *Studies on Fermentation: The Diseases of Beer, Their Causes, and the Means of Preventing Them*, trans. Frank Faulkner and D. Constable Robb (London, 1879)

Pawsey, Rosa K., *Case Studies in Food Microbiology for Food Safety and Quality* (London, 2007)

Robbins, Louise, *Louis Pasteur and the Hidden World of Microbes* (New York, 2001)

Sonnenburg, Justin, and Erica Sonnenburg, *The Good Gut: Taking Control of Your Weight, Your Mood, and Your Long-term Health* (New York, 2015)

Tamang, Jyoti Prakash, and Kasipathy Kailasapathy, eds, *Fermented Foods and Beverages of the World* (Boca Raton, FL, 2010)

Tattersall, Ian, and Rob DeSalle, *A Natural History of Wine* (New Haven, CT, 2015)

Toldrá, Fidel, ed., *Handbook of Fermented Meat and Poultry*, 2nd edn (Hoboken, NJ, 2014)

Tomes, Nancy, *The Gospel of Germs: Men, Women, and the Microbe in American Life* (Cambridge, MA, 1998)

Unger, Richard W., *A History of Brewing in Holland 900–1900: Economy, Technology and the State* (Leiden, 2001)

Valenze, Deborah M., *Milk: A Local and Global History* (New Haven, CT, 2011)

Vallery-Radot, René, *Louis Pasteur: His Life and Labours*, trans. Lady Claud Hamilton (New York, 1891)

Yong, Ed, *I Contain Multitudes: The Microbes within Us and a Grander View of Life* (New York, 2018)

Younger, William, *Gods, Men, and Wine* (Cleveland, OH, 1966)

# Acknowledgements

To the librarians and staff of Brown University's Rockefeller Library I owe my gratitude for their resourcefulness and patience in honouring my loan requests, which are often for obscure titles held in far-flung parts of the globe. My thanks and appreciation also go to my colleagues at Brown – Rebecca, John, Naomi, Trae, Kris, Jane, Liz and everyone else – whose words of encouragement sustained me as I researched and wrote this book.

For sustenance in those moments of leisure I allowed myself I thank Carrie Losneck, Chris Wright and Zack Barowitz, with whom I passed many pleasant weekends on Peaks Island. I'd especially like to thank Zack for his astute observation that it is the dwindling number of middle-class jobs that has driven the artisanal food movement to such heights of invention.

For editing and the countless other unglamorous jobs that go into preparing a manuscript, I thank Erwin Montgomery. Without his experience, learning, talent and intelligent involvement, this book wouldn't have been possible. And, of course, the folks at Reaktion have my gratitude as well.

I thank also the scholars whose work informs this book: Harvey Levenstein for his brilliant scholarship on the rise of the American food processing industry and the hygiene movement; Linda Civitello for her insightful work on the triumph of baking powder and how it changed the way we bake; John S. Marchant, Bryan G. Reuben and Joan P. Alcock for their engaging and informative account of the history of bread; Ian S. Hornsey and Richard Unger for their fascinating books on the history of beer and brewing; Nicholas P. Money for his many illuminating and always delightful books on fungi; and the many others listed in the endnotes. Finally, I thank Sandor Ellix Katz for his wonderful books on fermentation. They are an inspiration and a comfort.

# Photo Acknowledgements

The author and publishers wish to express their thanks to the below sources of illustrative material and/or permission to reproduce it:

Åbo Akademi: p. 56; Anonymous: p. 62; aperfectworld: p. 52; ayustety: p. 130; BabelStone: p. 22; Jean-Paul Barbier: p. 136; Biblioteca del Congreso Nacional: p. 19; Biodiversity Heritage Library: p. 132; Boston Public Library: pp. 91, 120; Bullenwächter: p. 183; Center for Disease Control: p. 176; Chidinma0025: p. 133; Captain Budd Christman, NOAA Corps: p. 172; Krish Dulal: p. 129; eheugenvannederland.nl: p. 13; FORTEPAN/Semmelweis Egyetem Levéltára: p. 125; Hajor: p. 24; Paul Hesse: p. 64; Paul de Kruif: p. 60; Library of Congress, Washington, DC: p. 177; Maulucioni y Doridí: p. 15; David E. Mead: p. 192; Miami University Libraries: p. 139; The National Archives, UK: p. 122; Dr Horst Neve, Max Rubner-Institut: p. 187; Otávio Nogueira: p. 166; Oregon State University: p. 181; Paxse: p. 174; Post of Kazakhstan: p. 143; Prado Museum: p. 170; Provincial Archives of Alberta: p. 8; Michael Rhode: p. 94; Science History Institute: p. 17; SMU Central University Libraries: p. 189; Y tambe: p. 182; Thesupermat: p. 98; Sonali Thimmiah: p. 106; United States Department of Agriculture: pp. 63, 96, 107; Paul VanDerWerf: p. 193; Digital Collection of the State Library of Victoria: p. 82; Wellcome Collection: pp. 36, 44; John Yesberg: p. 100; Zeyus Media: p. 185.

# Index